此专著由上海市浦江人才计划资助（17PJC010）
This book was sponsored by Shanghai Pujiang Program （17PJC010）

PRIMING AND ERP INVESTIGATIONS ON THE PROCESSING AND REPRESENTATION
OF THE TONAL ALTERNATIONS IN MANDARIN CHINESE AND SOUTHERN MIN DIALECT

基于启动和脑电波实验研究普通话和闽南语连续变调词的储存模式

钱昱夫 /著

復旦大學 出版社

Preface

This book aims to uncover the role of the acoustic input (the surface representation) and the abstract linguistic representation (the underlying representation) as listeners map the signal during spoken word recognition. To examine these issues, tone sandhi, a tonal alternation phenomenon in which a tone changes to a different tone in certain phonological environments, is investigated.

This book first examined how productive Mandarin tone 3 sandhi words (T3 → T2/___T3) are processed and represented. An auditory priming lexical decision experiment was conducted in which each disyllabic tone 3 sandhi target was preceded by a tone 2 monosyllable (surface-tone overlap), a tone 3 monosyllable (underlying-tone overlap), or an unrelated monosyllable (unrelated control). Lexical decision RTs showed a tone 3 (underlying-tone overlap) facilitation effect for both high and low frequency words.

A second priming study investigated the processing and representation of the more complex and less productive Southern Min tone sandhi. Lexical decision RTs, examining sandhi 24 → 33 and 51 → 55, showed that while both sandhi types exhibited facilitatory priming effects, underlying tone primes showed significantly more facilitation than surface primes for sandhi 24 → 33, while surface tone primes showed significantly more facilitation than underlying primes for sandhi 51 → 55, with both effects modulated by frequency.

A third study used event-related potentials (ERPs) to examine Mandarin tone 3 sandhi. Using an oddball paradigm, participants passively listened to either Tone 2 standards ([tṣu2 je4] /tṣu2 je4/), Tone 3 standards ([tṣu3 je4] /tṣu3 je4/), Tone Sandhi standards ([tṣu2 jen3] /tṣu3 jen3/), or Mix standards (i.e., both tone 3 sandhi and tone 3 words), occasionally interspersed with a tone 2 word [tṣu2] (i.e., the deviant). Results showed a mismatch negativity (MMN) in the Tone 2 condition but not in the Sandhi condition, suggesting different neural processing mechanisms for Tone 2 and Sandhi words.

Together, the current data suggest that the underlying tone contributes more to the processing of productive tone sandhi and the surface tone contributes more to the processing of less productive tone sandhi. In general, this book provides evidence for the representation and processing of words that involve phonological alternation, both within the same language and across different languages.

Table of Contents

Chapter 1 General Introduction 1
   1.0 Introduction 1
   1.1 Models of Spoken Word Recognition 7
      1.1.1 The Cohort Model 8
      1.1.2 TRACE 10
      1.1.3 Shortlist 12
      1.1.4 Neighborhood Activation Model 13
      1.1.5 Summary of Spoken Word Recognition Models 14
   1.2 Forms of Lexical Representations: Abstract vs. Episodic 15
   1.3 Research Questions 17
   1.4 Overview 19

Chapter 2 Priming the Representation of Mandarin Tone 3 Sandhi Words 21
   2.0 Introduction 21
   2.1 The Current Study 37
   2.2 Methods 38
      2.2.1 Subjects 38
      2.2.2 Stimuli 39
      2.2.3 Stimulus Recording 42
      2.2.4 Procedure 42
   2.3 Predictions 43
   2.4 Results 45
      2.4.1 Analysis of Variance (ANOVA) Analyses 45
         2.4.1.1 General Effect 45

		2.4.1.2	Error Analyses	49
		2.4.1.3	Facilitation Effect	50
		2.4.1.4	First Syllable Frequency Analyses	52
		2.4.1.5	Second Syllable Frequency Analyses	53
	2.4.2	Linear Mixed-Effects Model		53
2.5	Discussion			57
2.6	Conclusion			70

Chapter 3 Priming the Representation of Southern Min Tone Sandhi Words ········ 71

- 3.0 Introduction ········ 71
- 3.1 The Current Study ········ 76
- 3.2 Methods ········ 77
  - 3.2.1 Participants ········ 77
  - 3.2.2 Stimuli ········ 77
  - 3.2.3 Stimulus Recording ········ 79
  - 3.2.4 Procedure ········ 80
- 3.3 Results ········ 80
- 3.4 Discussion ········ 89
- 3.5 Conclusion ········ 94

Chapter 4 An ERP Study on Mandarin Tone 3 Sandhi Processing ········ 96

- 4.0 Neurophysiological Studies on Lexical Tone Processing ········ 96
- 4.1 The Current Mismatch Negativity Experiment ······ 105
- 4.2 Methods ········ 107
  - 4.2.1 Participants ········ 107
  - 4.2.2 Stimuli ········ 107
  - 4.2.3 Design ········ 108

	4.2.4 Procedure	113
	4.2.5 EEG Recordings	113
	4.2.6 Data Analysis	114
4.3	Predictions	116
	4.3.1 Onset	116
	4.3.2 Omission	118
4.4	Results	119
	4.4.1 Mean ERP Amplitude for the Onset and the First Syllable of Standards	119
	4.4.2 Mean ERP Amplitude for the Omission Position and the Second Syllable of Standards	126
4.5	Discussion	132
4.6	Conclusion	138

Chapter 5 General Discussion and Conclusion 139
- 5.0 Summary 139
- 5.1 Tone Sandhi Word Processing and Representation in the Mental Lexicon 140
- 5.2 Tone Sandhi Word Processing at a Very Early Stage of Language Comprehension 146
- 5.3 Models of Spoken Word Recognition 153
- 5.4 Conclusion 155

References 156

Appendix 1 Critical Target Mandarin Tone 3 Sandhi Stimuli 166

Appendix 2 Mandarin Disyllabic Filler Word Target Stimuli with Prime Words. Also, Disyllabic Nonword

　　　　　　　　　Target Stimuli with Prime Words ·············· 168

Appendix 3　Critical Target Southern Min Sandhi Stimuli
　　　　　　　·· 170

Appendix 4　Southern Min Disyllabic Filler Word Target
　　　　　　　Stimuli with Prime Words. Also, Disyllabic
　　　　　　　Nonword Target Stimuli with Prime Words
　　　　　　　·· 172

Appendix 5　Acoustic Details of the Seven Standard [tṣu2]
　　　　　　　Tokens, the Seven Standard [tṣu3] Tokens and
　　　　　　　the Deviant [tṣu2] (measured in Hz, rounded
　　　　　　　to the nearest integer) ···················· 175

List of Figures

Figure 1	The Fundamental Frequencies of the Four Mandarin Tones in /ma/	22
Figure 2	Tone 3 Sandhi Target [fu2 tao3] /fu3 tao3/ and Its Corresponding Primes	39
Figure 3	Mean Reaction Times (ms) and Error Bars for Tone 2, Tone 3, and Control Conditions in the Lexical Decision Task	46
Figure 4	Mean Reaction Times (ms) and Error Bars for High Frequency and Low Frequency Tone 3 Sandhi Targets in the Lexical Decision Task	47
Figure 5	The Linear Regression Line of Word Frequency and Reaction Time for All of the Tone 3 Sandhi Targets	48
Figure 6	Reaction Times (ms) and Error Bars in the Tone 2, Tone 3, and Control Conditions for High and Low Frequency Words	48
Figure 7	Error Rates in the Tone 2, Tone 3, and Control Conditions for High and Low Frequency Words	49
Figure 8	Facilitation Effects in the Tone 2 and Tone 3 Conditions for High and Low Frequency Words	51
Figure 9	Southern Min Tone Sandhi Circle (for Long Tones)	72
Figure 10	For Each Sandhi Target Type (51 → 55; 24 → 33), There Are Three Prime Conditions	79
Figure 11	Reaction Times (ms) and Error Bars in the Surface, Underlying, and Control Conditions for Words with Tone Sandhi 51 → 55 and Tone Sandhi 24 → 33	83

Figure 12 Facilitation Effects for the Surface and Underlying Prime Conditions (Relative to Baseline Control Condition) for Targets with Tone Sandhi 51 → 55 and 24 → 33 ·· 84

Figure 13 Facilitation Effects for Tone Sandhi 51 → 55 and 24 → 33 as a Function of Familiarity ················ 87

Figure 14 Stimuli in the Tone 2, Tone 3, Sandhi and Mix Conditions ·· 109

Figure 15 Average Fundamental Frequency Contour of the Seven Standard [tṣu2] Tokens and Fundamental Frequency Contour of the Deviant [tṣu2] ············ 111

Figure 16 Average Fundamental Frequency Contour of the Seven Standard [tṣu3] Tokens ·························· 112

Figure 17 Figure 17a, Figure 17b, Figure 17c and Figure 17d Depict Mean ERP Waveforms Averaged across 12 Participants in the 0-400 ms Time Window Using the -100-0 ms Time Window as the Baseline. Electrode FZ Was Selected ······························· 122

Figure 18 Figure 18a, Figure 18b and Figure 18c Depict Mean ERP Waveforms Averaged across 12 Participants in the 0-400 ms Time Window Using the -100-0 ms Time Window as the Baseline. Electrode FZ Was Selected ·· 124

Figure 19 Statistical Results of the Within-Condition Comparisons between the First Syllable of Standards and the Deviant in Each Condition as Well as the Statistical Results of the Between-Condition Comparisons for Deviants across Conditions. Asterisks Indicate Significant Effects and Trends ·························· 125

Figure 20	Figure 20a, Figure 20b, Figure 20c and Figure 20d Show Mean ERP Waveforms Averaged across 12 Participants in the 0–400 ms Time Window Using the −380–−280 ms Time Window as the Baseline. Electrode FZ Was Selected ··	128
Figure 21	Figure 21a, Figure 21b and Figure 21c Show Mean ERP Waveforms Averaged across 12 Participants in the 0–400 ms Time Window Using the −380–−280 ms Time Window as the Baseline. Electrode FZ Was Selected ··	130
Figure 22	Statistical Results of the Within-Condition Comparisons between the Second Syllable of Standards and the Omission in Each Condition as Well as the Statistical Results of the Between-Condition Comparisons for Omissions across Conditions. Asterisks Indicate Significant Effects and Trends ··	131

List of Tables

Table 1	Reaction Time Likelihood Ratio Tests: Model Comparisons	55
Table 2	Error Rate Likelihood Ratio Tests: Model Comparisons	57
Table 3	Southern Min Tones	72
Table 4	Reaction Time Likelihood Ratio Tests: Model Comparisons	81
Table 5	Reaction Time Likelihood Ratio Tests for Tone Sandhi 51 → 55: Model Comparisons	85
Table 6	Reaction Time Likelihood Ratio Tests for Tone Sandhi 24 → 33: Model Comparisons	86
Table 7	Error Rate Likelihood Ratio Tests: Model Comparisons	88

Chapter 1
General Introduction

1.0 Introduction

In order to understand utterances, listeners must recognize individual spoken words. Such a process is extremely complicated due to a number of reasons. First, a given word (e.g., [stil]) may have similar-sounding words (e.g., [stim], [stip], [stiɹ]), or be embedded in a longer word (e.g. [tʰɛn] in [ˈtʰɛnʃən]). Recognition of a word involves selection among competing words (Allopenna, Magnuson & Tanenhaus, 1998; Shen, Deutsch & Rayner, 2013; Salverda et al., 2007). Second, there is often no clear boundary between words in running speech. Speech is continuous and transitory, and it is difficult to segment continuous speech into individual words merely by locating pauses (Weber & Scharenborg, 2012). Third, speech is extremely variable. Sentences, words and phonemes vary in acoustic quality due to speaking rate, speaking style, talker and phonological environment (Goldinger, Pisoni, & Logan, 1991; Cheng, 1968). As a result, spoken word recognition is an extremely complicated process, yet listeners usually accomplish it without any difficulty.

With regard to phonological environment, American English /t/, for example, shows different acoustic realizations in different contexts (Reetz & Jongman, 2009). The phoneme /t/ is voiceless aspirated in the initial position of a stressed syllable, but voiceless unaspirated when preceded by a sibilant. Moreover, it changes into a voiced alveolar flap [ɾ] between a stressed and an unstressed vowel. Such a phenomenon shows how a phonological environment affects realizations of a segment (phoneme). The phonological environment also influences the phonetic realization of tones in tone languages (Wang & Li, 1967). For example, a Mandarin tone 3 syllable (a low-dipping tone) changes into a tone 2 syllable (a high-rising tone) when followed by another tone 3 syllable (a phenomenon known as Mandarin tone 3 sandhi). Given these phonological alternations, key questions arise as to how listeners segment words in speech and how they select the target word among a set of similar words. That is, how do listeners extract invariant information from a highly variable acoustic input? A further question is: how do listeners map acoustic-phonetic information of words onto their linguistic representations stored in the mental lexicon? This book aims to uncover the role of the acoustic input, or the surface representation, and that of the abstract linguistic representation, or the underlying representation, as listeners map the signal during spoken word recognition. Both psycholinguistic and neurolinguistic approaches will be used to examine Mandarin and Southern Min tone sandhi processing.

Issues of spoken word recognition have attracted intensive research in the fields of psycholinguistics and neurolinguistics. One of the most crucial findings concerning language comprehension is that listeners process speech incrementally (Stowe, 1986;

Kazanina et al., 2007; DeLong, Urbach, & Kutas, 2005; Federmeier, 2007; Bendixen et al., 2014). Studies have shown that listeners do not wait until the end of a word or a sentence to interpret speech. Instead, they actively posit several candidates simultaneously based on the incoming auditory information. Zwitserlood (1989) showed parallel activation of words in a semantic priming experiment in which presentation of the sound sequence [kæp] facilitated participants' lexical decision response times on "money" and "ship", which are semantically related to "capital" and "captain" respectively. The facilitation effect suggested that both "capital" and "captain" were activated in parallel after participants heard [kæp]. Tanenhaus, Spivey-Knowlton, Eberhard and Sedivy (1995) conducted an eye-tracking study and showed that participants spent a longer time matching a target object (e.g., candy) in a display with the auditorily presented stimulus (e.g., candy) when another object (e.g., candle) with a similar name was also present in the display than when there was no competing object, indicating that both the target and the competitor were considered simultaneously at the onset of the auditory stimulus presentation, and both were available until the incoming acoustic information allowed participants to disambiguate between the two objects.

Lexical activation is also influenced by acoustic-phonetic details of the input. If the input and the corresponding lexical representations match more closely, that set of words will be activated more strongly than if the input and the corresponding lexical representations have a greater mismatch. Whalen (1991) showed that the word "soup" was recognized faster when the formant transition of the initial [s] cued [u] than when it was manipulated to cue a different following vowel. Connine, Titone, Deelman and Blasko (1997) used a phoneme monitoring task to investigate whether the degree to which a word-initial segment matches its corresponding lexical representation would influence the speed of detecting the word's final voiceless stop. In their experiments, participants were asked to press a button as quickly and accurately as possible when hearing a voiceless stop. Stimuli were systematically manipulated such that one base word generated three corresponding nonwords: a minimal nonword (i.e., differing from its base word only at the initial consonant by an average of around 1.2 linguistic features), a maximal nonword (i.e., differing from its base word at the initial consonant by an average of around 5.8 linguistic features) and a control nonword (i.e., derived by changing all the segments of its base word except for the final vowel-consonant sequence). Results showed that participants' reaction times of detecting voiceless final stops were prolonged as the degree of match between the auditory stimuli and lexical representations decreased. These data suggest a gradation of lexical activation as a function of the goodness of match.

In addition to lexical activation, word candidates also compete with each other for recognition (McClelland & Elman, 1986; Norris, 1994; Luce & Pisoni, 1998). When a listener receives an input, a series of candidates which overlap with the input to some degree are activated, and lexical competition then occurs, with competing lexical candidates inhibiting each other.

The effect of lexical competition has been shown repeatedly. For example, McQueen, Norris, and Cutler (1994) observed that participants' reaction times increased when detecting a short word (e.g., sack) embedded in the onset of a longer word (e.g., [sækɹəf]), but decreased when searching for a short word embedded in the onset of a longer nonword (e.g., [sækɹək]). The result illustrates lexical competition between the short (e.g., sack) and long words (e.g., sacrifice), causing an increase in detection latency. Allopenna, Magnuson, and Tanenhaus (1998) conducted an eye-tracking study to demonstrate that not only do words sharing onset information compete with each other (e.g., beetle vs. beaker), but words overlapping in rhyme compete with each other as well (e.g., beetle vs. speaker), suggesting parallel activation of competing candidates during spoken word recognition. Furthermore, it has also been shown that lexical competition is modulated by the number of similar-sounding words being activated, with a dense neighborhood yielding stronger lexical competition and a sparse neighborhood eliciting weaker lexical competition (Vitevitch & Luce, 1998; 1999).

Apart from lexical competition that impacts spoken word recognition, sublexical information has also been shown to play a role in the word recognition process. Vitevitch & Luce (1998) showed that probabilistic phonotactics influenced spoken word recognition. In their experiment, participants heard auditorily presented words and were asked to repeat them as quickly and accurately as possible. Stimuli were categorized into four groups: words with high probabilistic phonotactics/neighborhood density, words with low probabilistic phonotactics/neighborhood density, nonwords with high probabilistic phonotactics/neighborhood density, and nonwords with low probabilistic phonotactics/neighborhood density. Results showed that words with high probabilistic phonotactics/neighborhood density elicited slower production reaction times than did words with low probabilistic phonotactics/neighborhood density. In contrast, nonwords with high probabilistic phonotactics/neighborhood density yielded faster production reaction times than did nonwords with low probabilistic phonotactics/neighborhood density. The authors interpreted these data as resulting from the interaction between lexical competition and sublexical cues, with the effect of lexical competition dominating that of sublexical facilitation. Since naming words involved accessing their lexical representations, words in a densely populated neighborhood competed with each other strongly, resulting in slower reaction times. Notice that although those words have a high phonotactic probability, the facilitation induced by higher sublexical activation did not overwhelm the effect of lexical competition. On the other hand, since nonwords do not possess lexical representations and therefore have much reduced lexical competition, the benefit of higher phonotactic probability emerged for nonwords with high probabilistic phonotactics/neighborhood density, resulting in faster production reaction times. Their data, thus, support models with both lexical and sublexical levels of processing in spoken word recognition.

A variety of spoken word recognition models have been proposed. In the following section, we will briefly introduce some of the most influential models of spoken word recognition, including the Cohort Model (Marslen-Wilson, 1978), TRACE (McClelland & Elman, 1986), Shortlist (Norris, 1994), and the Neighborhood Activation Model (Luce & Pisoni, 1998).

1.1 Models of Spoken Word Recognition

Models of word recognition were first developed for the recognition of written words. However, written and spoken word recognition undergo very different processes due to the nature of how humans perceive written and spoken words. Uniquely, models of spoken word recognition must acknowledge the temporal characteristic of speech, with the word onset being more prestigious than the word offset. Spoken models also need to tackle the fact that speech is continuous and transitory, and it is difficult to find a unit in speech that is completely independent of its adjacent units. Moreover, great variability induced by talker, speaking rate and phonological environment must be accounted for in models of spoken word recognition. Several spoken word recognition models were proposed in the 1980s and more have been established since then, such as the Cohort Model (Marslen-Wilson, 1978), TRACE (McClelland & Elman, 1986), Shortlist (Norris, 1994), and the Neighborhood Activation Model (Luce & Pisoni, 1998).

From a theoretical point of view, models of spoken word recognition differ from each other in their assumptions about the abstractness of representations both at the prelexical and lexical levels. Some models suggest more abstract representations than others. In addition, models of spoken word recognition are also different with respect to the direction of information flow. Interactive models allow information to not only flow from a lower level (i.e., acoustic-phonetic processing) to a higher level (i.e., lexical processing) (bottom up), but also descend from a higher level to a lower level (top down), while autonomous models only permit information to ascend from a lower level to a higher level (strictly bottom up). Debates on these issues still continue in the word recognition literature.

1.1.1 The Cohort Model

The Cohort Model is one of the first spoken word recognition models (Marslen-Wilson, 1978). Its seminal contribution is that it takes into account the temporal characteristic of spoken word processing by evaluating the acoustic-phonetic information of the input over time. The claims of this model have also motivated a number of more recent models.

In the Cohort Model, spoken word recognition undergoes three processes: lexical access, selection, and integration. At the stage of lexical access, acoustic-phonetic information of the input is evaluated over time, activating a set of word candidates, or cohort, that is matched with the input information. Candidates that are consistent with the input are activated simultaneously. Notice that the Cohort Model has a strictly temporal rule concerning word activation. That is, only word candidates whose onsets overlap with the input are activated and recruited into the cohort, meaning that offsets of words do not play any role. For example, after the initial 150-200 ms of the word "separate", the perceived sound sequence [sɛ] can only activate words beginning with this particular sequence, such as "set", "second", and "September", but not [pɛ], which only partially overlaps [sɛ]. After several word candidates are activated in parallel, the selection process commences. As more speech information unfolds, word candidates that are originally activated will be eliminated from the cohort if they mismatch the new speech input by more than one phonetic feature. Therefore, word candidate [sɛt] would be removed when the information of [p] comes in after [sɛ]. This process continues until only one candidate is left in the cohort. The selection process also allows that a word can be recognized before its offset if no other candidates overlap with it at a particular time point. During the final integration stage, word candidates' syntactic and semantic properties are evaluated with respect to the context. Any incongruency results in the removal of the candidates from the cohort, suggesting that higher-level constraints can affect word-level processing. In the original Cohort Model, lexical competition is not implemented; instead, recognition of spoken words is simply a process that continuously evaluates the degree to which word candidates match the input from the onset over time, with mismatched candidates being eliminated.

The traditional Cohort model has been challenged by some behavioral results in the psycholinguistics literature. Studies have shown that listeners can recover from a distorted acoustic signal and still recognize words, indicating that lexical representations can be accessed even though the input does not match them perfectly (Connine et al., 1997). Moreover, it has been demonstrated that few words can be uniquely distinguished before the offset of words (Luce, 1986), challenging Cohort Model's exclusive status of onset information of words. Subsequent models of spoken word recognition take some of these into consideration.

1.1.2 TRACE

TRACE (McClelland & Elman, 1986) is one of the first computational models of spoken word recognition. It is a localist model in which every single node is a representational unit. It is also a connectionist, interactive-activation model with three representational layers, i.e., a feature layer, a phoneme layer, and a word layer. The inputs that TRACE takes are composed of a variety of features. Words in this model are represented as strings of phonemes. In TRACE, the degree of match between the input and nodes is evaluated over time. Different nodes can be activated simultaneously, with those that more closely match the input being activated more strongly than those that match the input loosely. The input [sɛ], for example, will not only activate "set" and "separate", but also "onset" and "reset". Due to the parallel activation mechanism, unlike Cohort Model, words that match the offset of inputs can also be activated, showing that word recognition does not exclusively rely on word onset information.

Word recognition in TRACE is executed by an activation-competition process. Nodes matching inputs are activated and compete with each other in each layer. The node that best matches the input is most strongly activated, inhibiting the other candidate nodes. Competition among word candidates suggests that a word with more competing candidates should be recognized slower than a word with fewer competing candidates. There is no inhibition between nodes of different layers. Mismatching inputs do not lower the activation level of candidate words. With respect to the direction of information flow, the activation of feature nodes is spread to phoneme nodes, then to word nodes. Feedback from the word layer can also be sent down to the phoneme layer, making TRACE an interactive model, in that lexical information can affect listeners' phoneme perception.

In the original TRACE model, frequency was not explicitly modeled. Dahan, Magnuson, and Tanenhaus (2001) later proposed three ways for the TRACE model to incorporate this effect: by adjusting resting activation levels, by changing connection strengths, or by embodying this effect as a post-activation decision bias.

The time course of lexical activation is also captured by TRACE, which realizes it by mapping speech inputs continuously to lexical representations over time. Therefore, TRACE predicts that lexical activation of candidates overlapping the speech input in the onset position occurs earlier than those overlapping the speech input in the offset position. Such a prediction has been shown in the previous eye-tracking literature: listeners fixate onset competitors earlier and more than rhyme competitors (Allopenna, Magnuson, & Tanenhaus, 1998).

In addition, TRACE takes into consideration coarticulation among adjacent sounds during spoken word recognition by duplicating the entire network for every time slice, so that coarticulatory information can be captured by analyzing the overlapping speech input between adjacent segments as time proceeds. Although duplication allows the coarticulation properties to be modeled, the computational complexity that it introduces prevents the TRACE model to deal with large lexicons.

1.1.3 Shortlist

Shortlist (Norris, 1994) was designed to address the problem of duplication in TRACE and whether lexical feedback is needed during spoken word recognition (Norris, McQueen, & Cutler, 2000, 2003; Norris & McQueen, 2008; Magnuson, McMurray, & Tanenhaus, 2003; McQueen, 2003). It was claimed to be more parsimonious by its proponents in that it is a feed-forward model in which lexical feedback is not implemented. In Shortlist, spoken word recognition is structured via a two-stage process, i.e., a word candidate generation stage and a competition stage. In the first stage, a shortlist of word candidates (maximally 30) matching the speech input (a phoneme) so far is selected. Then, in the second stage, word candidates compete with each other in an interactive-activation network. Activation levels of individual word candidates are determined by the goodness of fit with the input. The word candidate that best matches the input gets activated most strongly, inhibiting the other competing word candidates. This whole recognition process repeats itself when each new phoneme becomes available, meaning that each input phoneme generates its own shortlist of word candidates and word layer in which candidates compete.

Similar to TRACE, lexical words in Shortlist are represented as phonemic strings, and words overlapping a given speech input both in the onset and offset positions can be activated. The effect of word frequency is not simulated in the original Shortlist. Shortlist B (Norris & McQueen, 2008), however, successfully incorporates this effect by treating word frequencies as prior probabilities. Different from TRACE, Shortlist can handle a more realistic size of lexicon (over 26,000 words) thanks to the two-stage design. In addition, Shortlist uses both segmental and suprasegmental information, namely lexical stress, to constrain lexical activation. Moreover, the Possible-Word Constraint implemented in Shortlist decreases the activation of a candidate word if the activation of that word makes its surrounding input a nonword. This is supported by psycholinguistic findings showing that it is much more difficult to detect "apple" in "fapple" (lower activation of apple) than in "vuffapple" (higher activation of apple) because "f" is not a viable English word but "vuff" is a possible word (Norris et al., 1997).

1.1.4 Neighborhood Activation Model

The neighborhood activation model (Luce & Pisoni, 1998), or NAM, is a model designed to evaluate effects of word frequency and number of similar-sounding words on spoken word recognition. Words in NAM are represented as acoustic-phonetic patterns. When an input comes in, a set of word candidates maximally differing from the input by a phoneme due to either substitution, deletion, or addition, will be activated. Activation is calculated by the goodness of fit between word candidates and the input. The activated acoustic-phonetic patterns of word candidates then activate word decision units, whose activation values are computed by the degree of fit between word candidates and the input, by their frequency-weighted neighborhood probabilities, and by the overall activity status of the word decision system. Finally, the word whose decision value exceeds a certain threshold will be recognized.

The NAM is important in theories of spoken word recognition in that it successfully simulates effects of neighborhood density and word frequency during spoken word recognition, as shown by the behavioral findings that words having less similar sounding words (neighbors) and high frequency are recognized faster than words having more neighbors and low frequency (Luce & Pisoni, 1998; Vitevitch & Luce, 1998).

1.1.5 Summary of Spoken Word Recognition Models

In the previous sections, we have reviewed some influential models of spoken word recognition. The list of models above is far from complete, focusing only on models of lexical processing, omitting models that emphasize speech sound perception (e.g., the LAFS model [Klatt, 1979]) and semantics (e.g., the semantic feature model [Smith, Shoben, & Rips, 1974] and the ACT model [Anderson, 1996]). Given that spoken word recognition models are usually developed to simulate a particular phenomenon in lexical processing, other effects in the word recognition process are often not clearly specified in the models. For example, it should be noted that the models mentioned above do not directly specify how words in tone languages, in which F0 (fundamental frequency) height and F0 contour are used to signal lexical identity, should be recognized. Therefore, it is difficult to conclude which model or models can better explain behavioral findings of spoken word recognition. Two of many controversies in the field now are information flow (top-down vs. bottom-up) and forms of stored representations (abstract vs. episodic). Issues of information flow concern whether lexical knowledge has a direct impact on pre-decisional pre-lexical processing (e.g., perception of phonemes). It has been acknowledged by both camps that designing a convincing study to uncover this issue is very difficult (McClelland, Mirman & Holt, 2006; McQueen, Norris & Cutler, 2006). With regard to lexical representations, it has been shown that neither extreme view concerning the form of lexical representations, purely abstract or episodic, is accurate. Lexical representations seem to incorporate both abstract and episodic information (Goldinger, 2007; Cutler & Weber, 2007; Norman & O'Reilly, 2003; Connine, Random, & Patterson, 2008). In the following section, we will briefly review these two representational views.

1.2 Forms of Lexical Representations: Abstract vs. Episodic

Many models of spoken word recognition, including those reviewed above, traditionally assume that lexical representations consist of abstract phonological codes that only preserve essential information for the recognition of spoken words, but omit surface acoustic-phonetic details resulting from speech rate, talker, and phonological alternation (McClelland & Elman, 1986; Norris, 1994; Luce & Pisoni, 1998). Variation in speech input is thus irrelevant in many spoken word recognition models and this variation is abandoned early before entering the encoding process.

Take the feature-based models of spoken word recognition as an illustration, such as TRACE and NAM. In these models, the elemental linguistic features of speech sounds are used in the recognition process. However, acoustic-phonetic details below the level of the linguistic features are still present in the input. A normalization process must operate to extract the information that is critical for word recognition. This process is considered economical for the lexicon because it does not need to store an infinite number of variable representations of words. Contrary to this abstractness account, Goldinger (1996, 1998) has proposed that surface acoustic-phonetic information does play a role in speech perception, and that surface physical details of words are stored in the mental lexicon rather than being discarded for a more abstract representation. For Goldinger, episodic representations of words are represented and preserved in memory.

Previous studies observed that listeners found it more difficult to recognize (Goldinger, 1996), identify (Mullennix, Pisoni & Martin, 1989), or recall (Goldinger, Pisoni & Logan, 1991) stimuli that were spoken by multiple talkers than by a single talker, indicating that surface acoustic-phonetic information does have an impact on lexical processing. However, the influence of surface acoustic details might vary for different levels of processing. For example, Goldinger

(1996) investigated effects of speakers' voices, delays between study and test sessions, and levels of processing in explicit and implicit memory during spoken word recognition. Listeners showed sensitivity to talkers' voices, indicating that voice attributes of spoken words were preserved in memory. Goldinger (1996) therefore concluded that surface details of the speech input are retained in the process of spoken word recognition. However, given that a large amount of evidence supports abstraction in speech perception, production and comprehension (Hintzman, 1986; Marsolek, 2004; Tenpenny, 1995), Goldinger (2007) proposed a *complementary systems* approach to account for the lexicon in which both abstract and surface information of the speech input is encoded in memory traces. He suggested that the abstract lexicon is necessary to interpret an exotic segment, while the episodic lexicon is needed to both generalize and delimit the effect. Other approaches propose two distinct storage mechanisms for abstract and surface representations (Schacter, 1992; Foder, 1983).

The present book will investigate the contribution of abstract and surface linguistic representations in spoken word recognition. It will also shed light on how words with mismatching underlying and surface representations (due to phonological alternations) are processed during spoken word recognition.

1.3 Research Questions

There are several research questions to address in this book. The first experiment uses a psycholinguistic approach to investigate how Mandarin speakers process Mandarin tone 3 sandhi words. Mandarin tone 3 sandhi is a tonal alternation phenomenon in which a tone 3 syllable changes into a tone 2 syllable when followed by another tone 3 syllable. Due to tone 3 sandhi, Mandarin tone 3 sandhi words' surface representation (i.e., [tone 2 tone 3]) mismatches their underlying representation (i.e., /tone 3 tone 3/). Given these differences, the first experiment addresses how Mandarin tone 3 sandhi words are represented in the mental lexicon. Are they represented based on their underlying representations or surface representations? And does frequency of occurrence affect the processing of Mandarin tone 3 sandhi words?

The second experiment examines the processing of Southern Min words with tone sandhi tone 51 → tone 55 and tone 24 → tone 33 (i.e., for Southern Min disyllabic words, the tone of the first syllable undergoes tone sandhi according to these two rules, and the tone of the second syllable stays unchanged). Similar to Mandarin, Southern Min tone sandhi words also exhibit a mismatching relationship between surface and underlying representations. Different from Mandarin tone 3 sandhi, Southern Min tone sandhi is more complicated, realizing itself in a circular chain-shift fashion. The second research question will address how Southern Min tone sandhi words are represented in the mental lexicon, and whether they are represented as their surface representations or underlying representations. The role of word frequency in the processing of Southern Min tone sandhi words is also to investigate.

The third experiment conductes a neurolinguistic study to

investigate the pre-attentive processing of Mandarin tone 3 sandhi words. By using a brain-imaging methodology, we will be able to directly measure how Mandarin speakers' brain handles the mismatch between surface and underlying representations at a very early stage of language processing.

Taken together, this book aims to uncover how tone sandhi words are represented in the mental lexicon, and whether it is the surface representation or underlying representation that is more influential during spoken word recognition. The psycholinguistic and neurolinguistic approaches used in this book will provide evidence at different stages of lexical processing. Results will shed light on how the human brain handles the mismatch between the two representations and whether it is necessary to posit an abstract linguistic representation to account for processing in spoken word recognition.

1.4 Overview

This book is divided into five chapters. Chapter 1 reviewes some classic models of spoken word recognition and different views concerning forms of lexical representations. Chapter 2 investigates the representations of Mandarin tone 3 sandhi words using an auditory-auditory priming lexical decision task. Chapter 3 examines the representations of Southern Min disyllabic words with tone sandhi 51 → 55 and 24 → 33 in an auditory-auditory priming lexical decision task. Chapter 4 investigates the pre-attentive processing of Mandarin tone 3 sandhi words using event-related potentials. Chapter 5 provides general discussions about the nature of representations of Mandarin and Taiwanese sandhi words and how our findings shed light on the models of spoken word recognition.

Chapter 2
Priming the Representation of Mandarin Tone 3 Sandhi Words

2.0 Introduction

Phonological alternations pose challenges to theories of lexical access and spoken word recognition. During the process of spoken word recognition, acoustic inputs map onto phonemes (or tonemes), and phonemes (or tonemes) onto words in speakers' mental lexicon. However, in real speech contexts, acoustic inputs do not always match their corresponding phonological representations in the speakers' mental lexicon in a straightforward way due to a variety of factors, such as coarticulation, speech rate, and phonological alternations. For phonological alternations, a phoneme is realized differently on the surface under certain circumstances. Mandarin tone 3 sandhi is an example of this incomplete match between surface representations and underlying representations.

Mandarin is a tone language where the pitch of syllables distinguishes word meanings. Syllables having the same segments but different tones have different lexical meanings. For example, /ma/ with tone 1 refers to "mother" (妈), while /ma/ with tone 2 means "hemp" (麻). Mandarin has four tones, including tone 1 (a high-level tone), tone 2 (a high-rising tone), tone 3 (a low-dipping tone), and tone 4 (a high-falling tone), as shown in Figure 1 below.

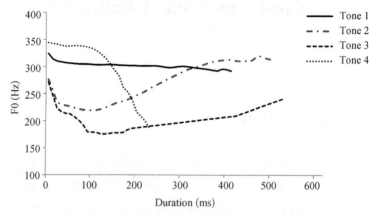

Figure 1 The Fundamental Frequencies of the Four Mandarin Tones in /ma/

There are a number of properties of Mandarin that are relevant to the processing of Mandarin words. First, compared to Indo-European languages, Mandarin shows a poverty of inflectional and derivational morphology (Li & Thompson, 1981). Second, Mandarin has a large number of compound words, consisting of approximately 73.6% by type and 34.3% by token in a corpus (Institute of Language Teaching and Research, 1986). The rest are mainly monomorphemic words, occupying 12.0% by type and 64.3% by token in the corpus. Last but not least, owing to the unbalanced numbers between Mandarin morphemes (around 6,000 morphemes) and Mandarin phonological forms of morphemes (about 1,300 different syllables, excluding accidental gaps), each Mandarin syllable corresponds to 4 morphemes on average, resulting in the phenomenon that a

Mandarin phonological form (a syllable) is very likely to have homophones. In extreme cases, the number of homophones of a syllable can reach 40 to 50.

Mandarin, as mentioned above, uses both segmental and tonal information to differentiate word meanings and this is of paramount importance in lexical access. Unlike most spoken word recognition models for Indo-European languages that focus on segments, Mandarin word recognition models must acknowledge both segmental and tonal information (Taft & Chen, 1992; Moore & Jongman, 1997; Ye & Connine, 1999; Zheng et al., 2012). To investigate word recognition in Mandarin, C.-Y. Lee (2007) used a direct priming task to examine how segmental and tonal information constrains Mandarin lexical activation. In the experiments, tonal and segmental information between primes and targets was manipulated. Four prime-target pairs were created for each target. In the first condition (ST), the prime and target were identical (e.g., lou2-lou2). In the second condition (S), the prime and target shared the same segmental information (e.g., lou3-lou2). In the third condition (T), the prime and target overlapped in terms of their tones (e.g., cang2-lou2). In the fourth condition (UR), the prime and target differed in both their tones and segments (e.g., pan1-lou2). The results showed that a significant facilitation effect was found when the prime and target were identical (ST), but no facilitation effect was found for the prime-target pairs differing only by tones (S) or by segments (T) relative to the control (UR). Based on his results, C.-Y. Lee (2007) concluded that both tonal and segmental information is used to constrain lexical activation with equal efficiency. However, Ye and Connine (1999) showed a modulation of monitoring effects as a function of the extent of tonal similarity. The lack of a facilitation effect for segmentally overlapping pairs in C.-Y. Lee (2007) might be confounded with the fact that the number of target tones presented was not controlled and the tonal distribution of prime-target pairs was not balanced across different conditions (Sereno & Lee, 2015).

Sereno and Lee (2015), following C.-Y. Lee (2007), investigated whether Mandarin tones and segments have the same status in constraining lexical activation by using a more well-controlled set of stimuli. Four identical conditions (ST, S, T, and UR) to those in C.-Y. Lee (2007) were used but the number of each target tone (tone 1, tone 2, tone 3, and tone 4) in each condition was balanced, so that the contribution of each of the four target tones across the prime conditions could be examined. The results showed a significant facilitation effect for the ST and S conditions and an inhibition effect for the T condition relative to the control condition (UR). Furthermore, the results of the S condition revealed that the reaction times were speeded when the offset F0 of the prime contrasted with the onset F0 of the target, such as a tone3-tone1 pair, and the response times were slowed when the offset F0 of the prime and the onset F0 of the target were comparable, such as a tone2-tone1 pair, implying that lower-level acoustic-phonetic information might contribute to the segmental priming effect. Sereno and Lee (2015) suggested that this contrast effect may be because a low F0 of a prime's offset makes the F0 of the target's onset sound higher. Consequently, a tone 1 target would be perceived more like a canonical tone 1 when following a tone 3 prime, which has a low F0 offset. A contrast effect in tone perception has also been shown in previous studies (Moore & Jongman, 1997; Sereno, Lee, & Jongman, 2011). Taken together, Sereno and Lee (2015) concluded that segmental information plays a more critical role in constraining Mandarin lexical activation than does tonal information and the nature of the tonal mismatch influences segmental priming, with similar F0 height between the offset of the primes and the onset of the targets harming lexical access when primes and targets are matched on segments.

In addition to the above mentioned studies investigating Mandarin monosyllabic words, it is worthwhile to examine how Mandarin disyllable words are processed since Mandarin has a large number of compound words. Zhou and Marslen-Wilson (1994) conducted auditory lexical decision experiments and used frequency differences among compound words as a diagnostic tool to explore how Mandarin semantically transparent compounds are processed. In the experiments, reaction times were measured in an experiment in which participants performed an auditory lexical decision task on disyllabic words and nonwords where word frequency, morpheme frequency, and syllable frequency were systematically manipulated, with either the first or the second constituent of the disyllabic words held constant. The results showed that disyllabic word frequency, rather than morpheme frequency, syllable frequency or the combination of these two, was the essential factor in influencing the subjects' lexical decision latencies, indicating Mandarin compound words may be represented as a whole. Although first-syllable frequency still played a role in shaping participants' reaction times during the lexical decision task when two compounds only differed by their first-syllable frequencies but were matched on their compound-word frequency, first-morpheme frequency, second-morpheme frequency, and second-syllable frequency, their data suggest that the internal morphological structure of Mandarin compounds only contributes to compound processing to a lesser extent.

Zhou and Marslen-Wilson (1995) conducted an auditory-auditory paired priming task and a repetition priming task to investigate how Mandarin compounds are represented in Mandarin speakers' mental lexicon. In the paired priming task, a disyllabic prime preceded a disyllabic target with no intervening items. In the repetition priming task, three versions were conducted: a short-lag version where the prime and the target were separated by 1 or 2 intervening items, a medium-lag version where the prime and the target were separated by 8-10 intervening items, and a long-lag version where 40-45 items intervened between the prime and the target.

In addition, five conditions were constructed for both of the paired priming and repetition priming tasks, where the prime and the target were exactly identical (identical condition), sharing the same morpheme (morphological condition), sharing the same syllable (homophone condition), having the same character but not the same morpheme (character condition), or totally unrelated (baseline condition). The constituent of the disyllables manipulated between the prime and the target could be the first constituent, the second constituent, or the second constituent of the prime and the first constituent of the target.

The results of both tasks showed that the identical and morphological conditions always elicited facilitation effects regardless of the number of intervening items between primes and targets, or the first or the second constituent of the disyllables that was manipulated. However, the facilitation effect was reduced when the primes and the targets were matched on their first constituent. Zhou and Marslen-Wilson suggested that the reduced facilitation effect was attributed to cohort competition on the word level, curtailing the facilitation effect resulting from re-activation of the recurring morphemes between primes and targets on the morpheme level. The homophone and character conditions elicited an inhibition effect when the prime and the target shared their first syllable, a facilitation effect when the prime and the target shared their second syllable, and a null effect when the second syllable of the prime and the first syllable of the target were matched. The authors proposed that the inhibition effect in the homophone and character conditions also resulted from cohort competition at the word level, while the facilitation effect observed in the four conditions when the second constituent of the primes and the targets were matched could be attributed to morpheme-level facilitation. The null effect found in the homophone and character conditions could be explained by the fact that word-level competition and morpheme-level facilitation cancelled each other out. They concluded that Mandarin compounds should be represented as a whole and their individual constituents should also be represented. They suggested that Mandarin speakers' mental lexicon might be organized as a multi-level hierarchical network, divided into feature, syllable, morpheme, and word levels of representations.

　　Mandarin disyllabic compound words can also undergo tonal alternation. There is a tonal alternation phenomenon called Mandarin tone 3 sandhi for Mandarin disyllabic compound words where the tone 3 (the low-dipping tone) syllable changes into a tone 2 (the high-rising tone) syllable when it is followed by another tone 3 syllable. For example, the lexical tone of the morpheme 保 /pɑw3/ ("to maintain") changes from tone 3 to tone 2 if it is followed by another tone 3 morpheme 险 /ɕjɛn3/ ("danger"). The surface representation of the tone 3 sandhi word 保险 ("insurance"), therefore, is [pɑw2 ɕjɛn3], rather than [pɑw3 ɕjɛn3]. When Mandarin speakers encounter a tone 2 syllable in speech, the tone 2 syllable may be either an underlying tone 2 or underlying tone 3 syllable. The tone 3 sandhi phenomenon raises questions regarding how Mandarin native speakers process tone 2 and tone 3 syllables during online processing, how tone 2 and tone 3 syllables map onto their phonological representations, and how Mandarin tone 3 sandhi words are represented in Mandarin native speakers' mental lexicon. Are the tones of the Mandarin tone 3 sandhi words represented as /tone 2 tone 3/ in native speakers' mental lexicon, or are they represented as /tone 3 tone 3/?

　　Zhou and Marslen-Wilson (1997) contrasted two views regarding how Mandarin tone 3 sandhi words are represented in

Mandarin speakers' mental lexicon, namely a "surface representation view" and a "canonical representation view" (Zhou & Marslen-Wilson, 1997). According to the surface representation view, the tones of Mandarin tone 3 sandhi words are represented as /tone 2 tone 3/ in the mental lexicon. That is to say, the tones that appear on the surface are stored directly as the underlying representation. In contrast, based on the canonical representation view, the tones of Mandarin tone 3 sandhi words are represented in the mental lexicon based on the concatenation of the citation forms of the constituent morphemes. Therefore, the Mandarin tone 3 sandhi words are represented as /tone 3 tone 3/ in speakers' mental lexicon. Mandarin tone 3 sandhi words then undergo a tone 3 sandhi rule, changing their first tone 3 syllables from an underlying tone 3 to a tone 2 on the surface.

Zhou and Marslen-Wilson (1997) used auditory-auditory priming lexical decision experiments to examine Mandarin tone 3 sandhi words in order to investigate the surface and canonical representation views. Two experiments were conducted. In their first experiment, thirty Mandarin tone 3 sandhi words were selected as critical targets (e.g., /tsʰaj3 tɕʰy3/ 采取 "to adopt"). Each tone 3 sandhi target was preceded by three kinds of disyllabic primes based on the tones of their first syllables, namely, a tone 2 prime (e.g., /tsʰaj2 xwa2/ 才华 "talent"), a tone 3 prime (e.g., /tsʰaj3 xoŋ2/ 彩虹 "rainbow"), and a control prime (e.g., /tʰjɛn1 ɤ2/ 天鹅 "swan"). The first syllable of the tone 2 prime matched the first syllable of the tone 3 sandhi target both on the segmental level and tonal level in the surface representation, while the first syllable of the tone 3 prime matched the first syllable of the tone 3 sandhi target both on the segmental level and tonal level in the underlying representation. In terms of the control prime, the first syllable of the control prime had no relationship with the first syllable of the tone 3 sandhi target, phonetically or semantically. In addition to the critical targets, another 30 disyllabic target nonwords served as fillers.

The results of their experiment 1 showed an inhibition effect (29 ms) in the tone 2 prime condition where the tone 2 primes yielded significantly slower reaction times than did the control primes. In contrast, a facilitation effect (52 ms) was found in the tone 3 prime condition where the tone 3 primes elicited significantly faster reaction times than did the control primes. Based on their results, Zhou and Marslen-Wilson (1997) suggested that the surface representation view was supported. They proposed that the inhibition effect obtained in the tone 2 prime condition was due to cohort competition on the word level between the tone 2 primes and the targets. The fact that tone 2 primes matched the initial syllables of the targets in the surface representation resulted in lexical competition. The authors also suggested that the facilitation effect observed in the tone 3 prime condition came from the fact that tone 3 primes activated all words starting with tone 3 syllables and their corresponding monosyllabic tone 3 morphemes, including those used as the first syllables of the tone 3 sandhi targets. After the presentation of the tone 3 sandhi targets, the pre-activated first tone 3 morphemes were boosted again, spreading the activation to the entire target word, resulting in a facilitation effect.

Zhou and Marslen-Wilson, however, also suggested that the canonical representation view could explain the results of their experiment 1, under the assumption of the strategic control of access processes (i.e., participants could develop strategies in the lexical decision task). Given strategic processes, they suggested that words beginning with a tone 2 syllable and words starting with a tone 3 syllable can both be activated in parallel after subjects heard the tone 3 sandhi targets because the tone 3 sandhi targets could activate words beginning with a tone 3 syllable in their underlying tone and words starting with a tone 2 syllable in their surface tone. After the presentation of tone 3 primes, the lexical access system would be biased toward a tone 3 interpretation with respect to the initial syllables of the sandhi targets. This tone 3 bias turned out to be beneficiary since the tone 3 interpretation of the first syllable of the sandhi targets matched exactly the underlying tone 3 of the first syllable of the sandhi targets, giving rise to the facilitation effect. As for the tone 2 primes, after the presentation, the lexical access system would be biased to a tone 2 interpretation with respect to the initial syllables of the sandhi targets. This tone 2 interpretation, however, turned out to be harmful because this interpretation cannot be mapped onto the first underlying tone 3 syllable of the sandhi targets, leading to processing burden, an inhibition effect.

In order to provide unambiguous evidence supporting one representational view over another, a second experiment, also using an auditory-auditory priming lexical decision task, was conducted (Zhou & Marslen-Wilson, 1997). Unlike the first experiment, all of the targets in the second experiment began with a tone 2 syllable, both in the underlying and surface representation. For each target (e.g., /tsʰaj2 pʰan4/ 裁判 "referee"), four primes were presented, namely, a tone 2 prime (/tsʰaj2 tʂʰan3/ 财产 "property"), a tone 3 prime (/tsʰaj3 xoŋ2/ 彩虹 "rainbow"), a sandhi prime (/tsʰaj3 tɕʰy3/ 采取 "to adopt"), and a control prime (/y4 ljaw4/ 预料 "to predict"). The first syllables of the tone 2 primes were homophonous to the first syllables of the targets. The first syllables of the tone 3 primes shared the same segments but not tones with the first syllables of the targets. The first syllables of the sandhi primes were homophonous to the first syllables of the targets in terms of their surface forms. The control primes were totally unrelated phonetically and semantically to the targets.

The results of the second experiment showed an overall inhibition effect in the tone 2 prime, tone 3 prime, and the sandhi prime conditions, with reaction times in these three conditions significantly slower than those in the control prime condition. In addition, the reaction times in the tone 2 prime (881 ms) and the sandhi prime (882 ms) conditions were comparable, but were significantly faster than those in the tone 3 prime condition (904 ms). Zhou and Marslen-Wilson suggested that the results in the second experiment were not consistent with the surface representation view or the canonical representation view.

According to the surface representation view, an inhibition effect would be expected in the tone 2 prime and the sandhi prime conditions because the primes and the targets shared the same segments and tones on the surface, leading to lexical competition on the word level. No inhibition effect would be expected in the tone 3 prime condition since there was no cohort competition between the primes and the targets whose initial syllables were tone 2.

According to the canonical representation view under the assumption of the strategic control of access processes, Zhou and Marselen-Wilson (1997) proposed that a facilitation effect would be expected for the tone 2 prime condition since the tone 2 primes would bias the processor toward the tone 2 interpretation for the first syllable of the targets, which exactly matched the tone of the first syllables of the targets (also a tone 2), resulting in a facilitation effect. In contrast, the sandhi primes should elicit an inhibition effect. When the processor received the sandhi primes, it would be biased toward a tone 3 interpretation for the first syllable of the targets when processing the targets because the underlying first tone 3 of the primes underwent the tone 3 sandhi rule. This tone 3 interpretation for the first syllable of the targets would not favor lexical access of the targets because the targets began with a tone 2 syllable. An inhibition effect would also be expected in the tone 3 prime condition, again, due to the fact that the processor had been biased toward a tone 3 interpretation for the first syllable of the targets after the presentation of the tone 3 primes; nonetheless, the first syllable of the targets was tone 2. Given that their data were not compatible with either of those two representational views, Zhou and Marslen-Wilson (1997) concluded that neither the surface representation view nor the canonical representation view is a possibility for how Mandarin speakers represent tone 3 sandhi words in their mental lexicon.

Zhou and Marslen-Wilson (1997) presented two possibilities for the representation of Mandarin tone 3 sandhi words. However, their data could not differentiate between the surface representation view and the canonical representation view. Moreover, a methodological concern in this study arises from the disyllabic primes. Since disyllabic primes were used in the auditory-auditory priming lexical decision task where the targets were presented right after the disyllabic primes, it is possible that the second syllable of the disyllabic primes might have played a role in the priming effects because the segmental and tonal overlap of the second syllable of the primes with the first syllables of the following targets is possible (stimuli not provided in Zhou & Marslen-Wilson, 1997). Third, since Mandarin compound words are represented as a whole and their individual morphemes may be represented as well (Zhou & Marslen-Wilson, 1995), it is hard to determine whether the priming effect, either inhibition or facilitation, is attributed to the individual morphemes of the disyllabic words, or to the disyllabic words as a whole. Last but not least, the effect of the lexical frequency of tone 3 sandhi words was not systematically varied in Zhou and Marslen-Wilson (1997). Lexical frequency may be a factor affecting the representation of Mandarin tone 3 sandhi words.

Zhang and Liu (2014), for example, investigated the productivity of Tianjin tone sandhi and found that words of higher frequency lead to higher tone sandhi productivity in

Tianjin Chinese. For example, their results of the sandhi pattern LH + LH → H + LH demonstrated that for the tone (H) of the first syllable of the sandhi words, high frequency words elicited higher F0, indicating that the sandhi raised the base tone (LH) more than the sandhi did to low frequency words in speech production (Zhang & Liu, 2014). This indicates that words of higher frequency had their surface H tone realized more closely to an underlying H tone than did words of low frequency. Zhang and Liu (2014) suggested that this result might be because high frequency words give rise to stronger lexical listing for the sandhi, realizing the sandhi pattern more thoroughly.

Yuan and Chen (2014), however, showed a different result for the realization of tone sandhi as a function of word frequency. Yuan and Chen (2014) investigated the acoustic characteristics of the first syllable of Mandarin tone 3 sandhi words in telephone conversation and broadcast news settings. Their results showed that the first syllable of higher frequency tone 3 sandhi words exhibited a smaller F0 rise than that of lower frequency tone 3 sandhi words, thus showing a greater difference between the tone 3 sandhi tone and an underlying tone 2 for high frequency words. In addition, there was a trend for the turning point of the F0 track to occur later for the first syllable of the higher frequency tone 3 sandhi words as compared to the lower frequency tone 3 sandhi words, indicating that the sandhi tone 2 of higher frequency words behaved more similarly to an underlying tone 3, whereas the sandhi tone 2 of lower frequency words was more like an underlying tone 2. These data suggest that Mandarin tone 3 sandhi was realized more completely for low frequency words.

The difference in the patterning of high and low frequency sandhi tones above might be due to the nature of the tasks used in the two studies. In Zhang and Liu (2014), participants were presented with two monosyllables auditorily with an 800 ms interval between them and were asked to put these two monosyllables together and pronounce them as a real disyllabic word in Tianjin Chinese. Therefore, participants were given the base tone of the disyllabic words before they pronounced them. In Yuan and Chen (2014), spontaneous speech of telephone conversations as well as broadcast news were used, with tone 3 sandhi words occurring in natural conditions. Given their results, it appears that it is easier for speakers to access the underlying representation of low frequency words when the base tones of words are provided, as in Zhang and Liu (2014), while it is easier for speakers to access the underlying form of high frequency words during spontaneous speech, as in Yuan and Chen (2014). Although the patterns of the effect of lexical frequency in these two studies differed, lexical frequency *did* contribute to the realizations of sandhi tones across Chinese languages.

Based on these findings, the effect of word frequency on the representation of Mandarin tone 3 sandhi words could be in one of two directions. Based on Zhang and Liu (2014), it may be possible that the Mandarin tone 3 sandhi rule is more productive for high frequency words than for low frequency words, with Mandarin speakers more sensitive to the surface representations for high frequency Mandarin tone 3 sandhi words compared to low frequency Mandarin tone 3 sandhi words. Based on Yuan and Chen (2014), an opposite hypothesis can be proposed, which states that Mandarin speakers may be more sensitive to the surface representations for low frequency Mandarin tone 3 sandhi words relative to high frequency ones. Given these data, it seems warranted to further investigate frequency differences in the processing of tone 3 sandhi words in Mandarin.

2.1 The Current Study

The aim of this present study is to investigate how Mandarin tone 3 sandhi words are represented in Mandarin speakers' mental lexicon and whether word frequency plays a role in determining how tone 3 sandhi words are stored and accessed. An auditory-auditory priming lexical decision task was used as a diagnostic tool to directly examine the influence of monosyllabic primes on disyllabic tone 3 sandhi targets. The surface representation view and canonical representation view will be tested to see whether Mandarin native speakers are more sensitive to the surface representations of the tone 3 sandhi words ([tone 2 tone 3]), or are more sensitive to the underlying representations of the tone 3 sandhi words (/tone 3 tone 3/).

In addition, based on the lexical frequency effect on tone sandhi in Zhang and Liu (2014) as well as Yuan and Chen (2014), it may be possible that word frequency influences the way in which Mandarin native speakers weigh the representation of Mandarin tone 3 sandhi words. Hence, two sets of hypotheses were made concerning frequency of occurrence. First, according to the frequency effect data of Zhang and Liu (2014), we hypothesize that for high frequency tone 3 sandhi words, their surface representations ([tone 2 tone 3]) may be weighed more heavily because they are frequently used, with tone 2 surfacing more often, the tone 3 sandhi rule is expected to be applied more completely, and native Mandarin speakers may be more sensitive to those words' surface representations rather than their underlying representations during online processing. For low frequency tone 3 sandhi words, their underlying representations (/tone 3 tone 3/) may be weighed more heavily since they are not frequently used and the tone 3 sandhi rule may not be applied that completely and native Mandarin speakers may be more sensitive to their underlying representations rather than their surface representations during spoken word recognition. Conversely, based on the result of lexical frequency in Yuan and Chen (2014), we hypothesize a reverse pattern for the representations of high frequency and low frequency Mandarin tone 3 sandhi words, with high frequency tone 3 sandhi words' underlying representations (/tone 3 tone 3/) weighed more heavily, and low frequency tone 3 sandhi words' surface representations (/tone 2 tone 3/) weighed more heavily.

2.2 Methods

2.2.1 Subjects

Thirty-three native Mandarin speakers (28 male, 5 female) living in Taiwan were recruited in this study. None of them had any reported language impairments or cognitive disabilities. Their ages ranged from 20 to 32 years old at the time of testing.

2.2.2 Stimuli

Thirty disyllabic tone sandhi words were selected as critical targets. They were all chosen from a corpus entitled Digital Resources Center for Global Chinese Teaching and Learning (Chin-Chuan Cheng, Chu-Ren Huang, Feng-Ju Lo, Mei-Chih Tsai, Yun-Chun Huang, Xiang-Yu Chen, Joyce Ya-Chi Han, and Chi-Jung Lu, 2005). Each tone sandhi target was preceded by one of the three corresponding monosyllabic primes, i.e., a tone 2 prime, a tone 3 prime, and a control prime (see Figure 2). Each tone sandhi target's first syllable overlapped with its corresponding tone 2 prime both on the segmental level and on the tonal level in the surface representations, while each tone sandhi target's first syllable overlapped with its corresponding tone 3 prime both on the segmental level and on the tonal level in the underlying representations. Each tone sandhi target's first syllable was different from its corresponding control prime (a tone 1 syllable) only in terms of tone, both in the surface representation and in the underlying representation.

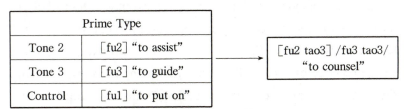

Figure 2 Tone 3 Sandhi Target [fu2 tao3] /fu3 tao3/ and Its Corresponding Primes

Among the tone sandhi targets, 15 of them were high frequency tone 3 sandhi words, with a mean word frequency of 898/5 million (SD = 566), a mean log-transformed word frequency of 2.88 (SD = 0.23), a mean log-transformed first syllable frequency of 3.18 (SD = 0.29) (i.e., defined as the sum of the homophones' frequencies either as a tone 2 or as a tone 3 syllable for the first syllable of the tone 3 sandhi targets), and a mean log-transformed second syllable frequency of 2.97 (SD = 0.36) (i.e., defined as the sum of the homophones' frequencies of the second syllable of the tone 3 sandhi words). Fifteen of them were low frequency tone 3 sandhi words, with a mean word frequency of 24/5 million (SD = 13), a mean log-transformed frequency of 1.32 (SD = 0.21), a mean log-transformed first syllable frequency of 3.04 (SD = 0.34), and a mean log-transformed second syllable frequency of 2.90 (SD = 0.38). All of the critical targets, their log-transformed word frequencies, log-transformed first syllable frequencies, and log-transformed second morpheme frequencies are displayed in Appendix 1.

In addition to the tone 3 sandhi targets, 60 filler disyllabic words were selected from the same corpus. These 60 filler target words were included so that participants would be less likely to develop strategic processing in the auditory-auditory priming lexical decision task. For the 60 disyllabic words, 11 of them were preceded by monosyllabic primes having the same tone and the same segment as the first syllable (ST match) (e.g., guan1-guan1men2, yan2-yan2liao4, ran3-ran3se4, and fan4-fan4wan3). The numbers of the tones of the first syllables of the 11 targets were 2 for tone 1, 3 for tone 2, 3 for tone 3, and 3 for tone 4. Thirteen of the 60 disyllabic words were preceded by the monosyllabic primes sharing only segments but not tones with the first syllables of their corresponding targets (S match) (e.g., mao1-mao3ding1, shu2-shu3tiao2, and da4-da1che1). The remaining 36 disyllabic targets were preceded by the monosyllabic primes sharing neither segments nor tones with the first syllable of their corresponding targets (ST mismatch) (e.g., tou1-ba2guan4, hong2-ji1ben3, qiang3-shui4jiao4, and dong4-ting1ke1). The numbers of tones of the first syllables of those 36 disyllabic targets were balanced, with 9 for each of the four tones. The filler target words are shown in Appendix 2.

Ninety disyllabic nonwords consisting of two legal monosyllables in Mandarin were also included. The combinations of the two monosyllables were not Mandarin words (i.e., accidental gaps). Among the 90 disyllabic nonwords, 21 of them were preceded by the monosyllabic primes having the same segment and tone as the first syllables of their corresponding targets (ST match); 33 of them were preceded by the monosyllabic primes having only the same segments but not tones as the first syllables of their corresponding targets (S match); 36 of them were preceded by the monosyllabic primes sharing nothing in common on either the segmental level or on the tonal level with the first syllables of their corresponding targets (ST mismatch). The nonword stimuli are shown in Appendix 3. For the 90 disyllabic nonword targets, 22 of them began with a tone 1 syllable; 22 of them began with a tone 2 syllable; 23 of them began with a tone 3 syllable; 23 of them began with a tone 4 syllable. For the 90 monosyllabic primes of those targets, 23 of them were tone 1; 22 of them were tone 2; 22 of them were tone 3; 23 of them were tone 4.

2.2.3 Stimulus Recording

A female native Taiwan Mandarin speaker was asked to produce all of the stimuli. The stimuli were recorded in an anechoic chamber with a cardioid microphone (Electrovoice, model N/D767a) and a digital solid-state recorder (Marantz, model PMD671), using a sampling rate of 22,050 Hz at the University of Kansas. All of the stimuli produced by the speaker were used either for the main experiment or for the practice section in this study.

2.2.4 Procedure

An auditory-auditory priming lexical decision experiment was conducted. Participants were first asked to fill out a questionnaire regarding their language background and sign a consent form. Then they were invited to a quiet room and were seated in front of a computer. All of the stimuli in the experiment were presented randomly over headphones (Beats Executive Over-Ear Headphones) using Paradigm (Tagliaferri, 2005). Twenty practice trials were presented first and then the 180 main trials.

For the 180 main trials, 30 of them were critical trials and were presented with a Latin Square design, such that each participant would only hear a critical target (a tone 3 sandhi target) once, preceded by either its corresponding tone 2 prime, tone 3 prime, or control prime. The remaining 150 trials were shared across all participants.

On each trial, participants heard a monosyllabic prime first. After a 250 ms interval (ISI), they heard a disyllabic target, either a word or a nonword. The participants' task was to judge whether the disyllabic target was a real word or a nonword by clicking the left button, representing "yes", or the right button, representing "no", of the mouse as quickly and accurately as possible. All of the participants used their dominant hand to make their responses. The ITI (intertrial interval) was 3,000 ms. Reaction times and errors obtained from the lexical decision task were subjected to statistical analyses. The duration of the experiment was about 20 minutes.

2.3 Predictions

If Mandarin tone 3 sandhi words are represented as surface representations, then the tone 2 primes should yield faster reaction times than tone 3 primes. However, if Mandarin speakers access the underlying representations of the tone 3 sandhi words, then the tone 3 primes should elicit faster reaction times than tone 2 primes. With respect to a main effect of frequency, high frequency tone 3 sandhi targets should produce overall faster reaction times than low frequency tone 3 sandhi targets. With regard to an interaction effect, based on Zhang and Liu (2014) showing that speakers were easier to access the underlying form of low frequency tone sandhi words than that of high frequency tone sandhi words when base tones of words were given, it is possible that for high frequency tone 3 sandhi words, tone 2 primes may elicit faster reaction times than tone 3 primes, while for low frequency tone 3 sandhi words, tone 3 primes may yield faster reaction times than tone 2 primes. However, the interaction effect can also be predicted in the reverse fashion based on Yuan and Chen (2014), which demonstrated that speakers were easier to access the underlying representation of high frequency tone 3 sandhi words than that of low frequency tone 3 sandhi words in spontaneous speech, with tone 2 primes eliciting faster reaction times than tone 3 primes for low frequency tone 3 sandhi words, and tone 3 primes yielding faster reaction times than tone 2 primes for high frequency tone 3 sandhi words.

Furthermore, since control primes do not share the same tone with the first syllable of the tone 3 sandhi targets, it is expected that these control primes will elicit the slowest reaction times among the three prime conditions across both frequency targets, namely, facilitation effects will be expected across both Tone 2 and Tone 3 conditions. Finally, no inhibition effect resulting from cohort competition at the word level is predicted in the Tone 2 and Tone 3 conditions compared to the Control condition. Since Mandarin has a large number of compound words (Li & Thompson, 1981) and monosyllabic content words are rarely used individually in Modern Chinese, it is very likely that Mandarin monosyllables are accessed as the morphemes used in compound words. As a result, after hearing a monosyllabic prime, Mandarin participants may take advantage of a set of pre-activated morphemes on the morpheme level to help them access the corresponding tone 3 sandhi targets.

2.4 Results

2.4.1 Analysis of Variance (ANOVA) Analyses

2.4.1.1 General Effect

Statistical analyses were conducted on both the reaction times and the log-transformed reaction times. Both analyses showed identical results. The log-transformed analyses are presented below. To facilitate presentation, all reaction times and graphs are displayed with untransformed values. Statistical analyses were also conducted for the error data.

All thirty-three subjects' data in the lexical decision task were included in the statistical analyses, with an overall mean accuracy of 91.57% (SD = 3.84%) (5,439 trials/5,940 trials). For the reaction time analyses, incorrect responses to the tone 3 sandhi targets (55 trials/990 trials) and responses to the tone 3 sandhi targets over two standard deviations either above or below each subject's mean (16 trials/990 trials) were excluded from the analyses. For the error analyses, error rates for all critical items were subjected to statistical analyses as well.

For the reaction time data, a 3 by 2 repeated-measures analysis of variance (ANOVA) was conducted where Prime (3 levels) and Frequency (2 levels) were set as independent variables. Both subject and item analyses were conducted on the log-transformed reaction times. For the subject analysis, both Tone and Frequency were within-subjects variables while for the item analysis, Tone was a within-subjects variable and Frequency a between-subjects variable.

The reaction time analyses showed there was a main effect of Prime ($F1(2, 64) = 21.100$, $p < .001$; $F2(2, 56) = 13.252$, $p < .001$). As displayed in Figure 3, pairwise comparisons for Prime illustrated that the mean reaction time for the Tone 3 condition was significantly faster than that for the Tone 2 condition both by subjects ($p < .001$) and by items ($p < .001$), with a difference of 88 ms. The mean reaction time for the Tone 3 condition was also significantly faster than that for the Control condition both by subjects ($p < .001$) and by items ($p < .001$), differing by 103 ms. No significant reaction time difference was observed between the Tone 2 and Control conditions, either by subjects ($p = .590$) or by items ($p = .616$).

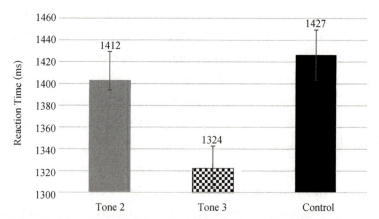

Figure 3 Mean Reaction Times (ms) and Error Bars for Tone 2, Tone 3, and Control Conditions in the Lexical Decision Task

There was also a main effect of Frequency ($F1(1, 32) = 14.301$, $p = .001$; $F2(1, 28) = 3.899$, $p = .058$), indicating that there was a significant reaction time difference between high and low frequency tone 3 sandhi targets in the lexical decision task. As shown in Figure 4, high frequency words were on average 63 ms faster than low frequency words.

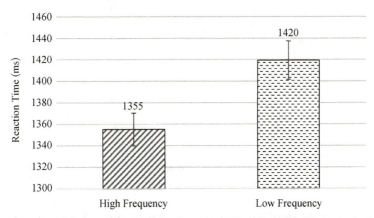

Figure 4　Mean Reaction Times (ms) and Error Bars for High Frequency and Low Frequency Tone 3 Sandhi Targets in the Lexical Decision Task

A linear regression analysis was also conducted on all of the tone 3 sandhi targets where log-transformed Frequency was set as an independent variable and log-transformed reaction time was designated as a dependent variable. The results confirmed the Frequency effect obtained by the ANOVA analysis, showing that word frequency and reaction time were significantly negatively correlated with each other ($t(28) = -2.409$, $p = .023$). Word frequency is a good predictor of subjects' reaction times in the lexical decision task, as shown in Figure 5. As word frequency increased, subjects' reaction times decreased.

The Prime X Frequency interaction effect was not significant ($F1(2, 64) = .204$, $p = .816$; $F2(2, 56) = .438$, $p = .648$), indicating that reaction time patterns for the Tone 2, Tone 3,

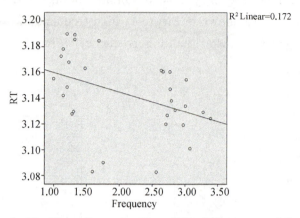

Figure 5 The Linear Regression Line of Word Frequency and Reaction Time for All of the Tone 3 Sandhi Targets

and Control conditions were not significantly different across the two Frequency conditions. Figure 6 shows participants' overall mean reaction times in the Tone2, Tone3, and Control conditions as a function of high and low frequency words.

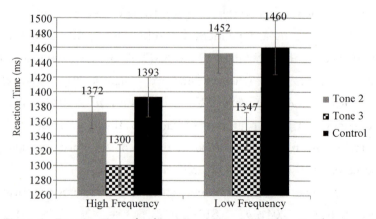

Figure 6 Reaction Times (ms) and Error Bars in the Tone 2, Tone 3, and Control Conditions for High and Low Frequency Words

2.4.1.2 Error Analyses

A 3 by 2 repeated-measures analysis of variance (ANOVA) was also conducted on the error rates (dependent variable) where Prime (3 levels) and Frequency (2 levels) were set as independent variables. Both subject and item analyses were conducted on the error data. For the subject analysis, both Prime and Frequency were treated as within-subjects variables while for the item analysis, Prime was set as a within-subjects variable and Frequency was regarded as a between-subjects factor. The overall error rate data are shown in Figure 7 below.

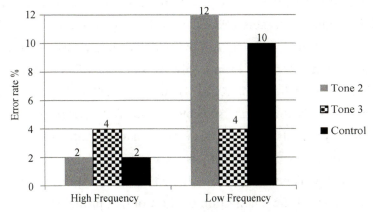

Figure 7 Error Rates in the Tone 2, Tone 3, and Control Conditions for High and Low Frequency Words

The results of the error rate data showed no main effect of Prime ($F1(2, 32) = 1.140$, $p = .326$; $F2(2, 28) = .867$, $p = .426$), indicating that error rates were similar across the three Prime conditions. A main effect of Frequency ($F1(1, 32) = 31.189$, $p < .000$; $F2(1, 28) = 4.228$, $p = .049$) was obtained, illustrating that low frequency tone 3 sandhi targets produced higher error rates than did high frequency tone 3 sandhi targets. A Prime X Frequency interaction effect ($F1(2, 32) = 4.710$, $p = .012$; $F2(2, 28) = 2.575$, $p = .085$) was also observed by subjects and a trend towards significance by items, showing that error rates in the three Prime conditions patterned slightly differently as a function of word frequency. Due to the interaction effect, two separate one-way ANOVAs were conducted on the error rates of high frequency tone 3 sandhi targets and low frequency tone 3 sandhi targets, individually. For the high frequency targets, the Tone 2, Tone 3 and Control conditions did not result in significantly different error rates across conditions, reflected by the fact that high frequency targets elicited very low error rates across all tone conditions, whereas for the low frequency targets, there was a main effect of Prime only by subjects ($F1(2, 98) = 3.779$, $p = .026$; $F2(2, 44) = 1.109$, $p = .339$). The statistical analyses indicated that subjects made few errors to high frequency targets overall, while they made significantly more errors to low frequency targets. Also, for the low frequency targets, the Tone 3 condition elicited significantly fewer errors than did the Tone 2 condition or the Control prime condition.

2.4.1.3 Facilitation Effect

In addition to the analyses mentioned above, analyses on the facilitation effect compared to the baseline Control condition were also conducted across the two different frequency groups. Log-transformed reaction times for the Tone 2 and Tone 3 conditions were subtracted from those in the Control condition to assess the facilitation effect.

There was a main effect of Prime ($F1(1, 32) = 32.528$,

$p < .001$; $F2(1, 28) = 18.261$, $p < .001$), which indicated that the facilitation effect yielded by tone 3 primes (103 ms) was significantly stronger than that elicited by tone 2 primes (14 ms), with a difference of 89 ms.

There was no main effect of Frequency ($F1(1, 32) = .013$, $p = .911$; $F2(1, 28) = .124$, $p = .728$). A frequency effect (high frequency words = 56 ms; low frequency words = 61 ms) was not expected given the fact that facilitation effects were derived by calculating the reaction times in the Tone 2 and Tone 3 conditions relative to those in the Control condition, which was matched to each frequency group.

Finally, no interaction effect was found ($F1(1, 32) = .679$, $p = .416$; $F2(1, 28) = .792$, $p = .381$), which indicated that the patterns of the facilitation effects between the Tone 2 and Tone 3 conditions for high and low frequency words were not significantly different (see Figure 8).

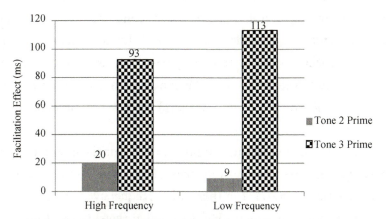

Figure 8 Facilitation Effects in the Tone 2 and Tone 3 Conditions for High and Low Frequency Words

To sum up, a main effect of Prime but no main effects of Frequency or a Prime X Frequency interaction illustrated that the facilitation effects of Prime were consistent across Frequency. Facilitation effects for the Tone 3 condition were significantly stronger than those for the Tone 2 condition across both high and low frequency words.

2.4.1.4 First Syllable Frequency Analyses

In the following two sections, several regression analyses were conducted to examine the contribution of first syllable frequency and second syllable frequency to the reaction time data. First syllable frequencies of the tone 3 sandhi targets were calculated based on the corpus entitled "Hong Kong, Mainland China & Taiwan: Chinese Character Frequency — a Trans-Regional Diachronic Survey" (Ho et al., 2001). First syllable frequency was defined as the total number of the homophones' frequencies either as a tone 2 or as a tone 3 syllable for the first syllables of the tone 3 sandhi targets (shown in Appendix 1). Two linear regression analyses were conducted on the high and low frequency words where First Syllable Frequency (the log-transformed syllable frequency) was set as an independent variable and Reaction Time (mean log-transformed reaction times to the tone 3 sandhi targets) was set as a dependent variable.

The regression results did not show a significant correlation between the first syllable frequency of the tone 3 sandhi targets and reaction times for either high frequency tone 3 sandhi targets or low frequency tone 3 sandhi targets, indicating that the first syllable frequency of the tone 3 sandhi words was not a good predictor of the reaction times obtained in the lexical decision task (high frequency words: $r = .201$, $p = .473$; low frequency words: $r = .285$, $p = .304$).

2.4.1.5 Second Syllable Frequency Analyses

Second syllable frequencies of the tone 3 sandhi words were calculated in accordance with the corpus entitled "Hong Kong, Mainland China & Taiwan: Chinese Character Frequency — a Trans-Regional Diachronic Survey" (Ho et al., 2001). Second syllable frequency of the tone 3 sandhi words was defined as the sum of the homophones' frequencies of the second syllable of the tone 3 sandhi words. Linear regression analyses were conducted where Second Syllable Frequency (the log-transformed syllable frequency) was regarded as an independent variable and Reaction Time (mean log-transformed reaction times to the tone 3 sandhi targets) was set as a dependent variable.

The regression results showed no significant correlation for high and low frequency tone 3 sandhi targets, respectively (high: $r = -.158$, $p = .574$; low: $r = .256$, $p = .357$), demonstrating that second syllable frequency was not a good predictor of reaction times for high and low frequency tone 3 sandhi words. Thus, neither first syllable nor second syllable frequency dictated subjects' reaction times during lexical access in the lexical decision task in this study.

2.4.2 Linear Mixed-Effects Model

Linear mixed-effects analyses were also conducted on participants' log-transformed reaction times using the lme4 package in R (Bates et al., 2014). The dependent variable in the analyses was subjects' log-transformed reaction times to the tone 3 sandhi targets in the lexical decision task. The fixed variables in the model were Prime (Tone 2, Tone 3, Control), and Frequency (i.e., log-transformed word frequencies of the tone 3 sandhi targets). These analyses were conducted where Frequency was considered a continuous independent variable rather than a categorical (i.e., high vs. low frequency words) variable to supplement the previous ANOVA analyses where Frequency was treated as categorical. Subject and item in this model were treated as random variables. The Control condition was chosen as the baseline to which the Tone 2 and Tone 3 conditions were compared.

Results of log-transformed reaction times from the linear mixed-effects analyses were identical to those from the previous ANOVA analyses. The results generated by the model showed significantly faster reaction times for the Tone 3 condition relative to the Control condition, $t(915) = -6.36$, $p < .0001$, but no reaction time differences for the Tone 2 condition when compared to the Control condition, $t(915) = -.10$, $p = .920$. It also revealed a significant effect of Frequency, $t(915) = -2.32$, $p = .020$, indicating that subjects' reaction times decreased as word frequencies increased. These results demonstrate a facilitatory priming effect for the Tone 3 condition and a frequency effect, which is consistent with the results shown in the ANOVA analyses.

After confirming the significant main effects of Prime and Frequency using the model above (Model A), a series of likelihood ratio tests was conducted to examine the effect of First syllable frequency (FSFreq), Second syllable frequency (SSFreq), as well as the interaction of Prime and Frequency where subjects' log-transformed reaction times was treated as a dependent variable, and subject and item were regarded as random variables. Results of likelihood ratio tests showed no effect of First syllable frequency by comparing Model B with Model A, no effect of Second syllable frequency by comparing Model C and Model B, and no effect of Prime X Frequency interaction by comparing Model D with Model C, as displayed in Table 1. The analyses demonstrated that the more complex models could not explain more variance of the reaction time data, indicating that the additional parameters, namely, First syllable frequency, Second syllable frequency, and the Prime X Frequency interaction, did not contribute much to the models. Therefore, we concluded that Model A was the best-fitting model to our reaction time data and the statistical results generated by this model were consistent with those from the subject and item ANOVAs.

Table 1 Reaction Time Likelihood Ratio Tests: Model Comparisons

Model	Factor 1	Factor 2	Factor 3	Factor 4	Factor 5
A	Prime	Freq	N/A	N/A	N/A
B	Prime	Freq	FSFreq	N/A	N/A
C	Prime	Freq	FSFreq	SSFreq	N/A
D	Prime	Freq	FSFreq	SSFreq	Prime X Freq

Model Comparison	χ^2	Df	p value
B vs. A	0	1	p = 1
C vs. B	0	1	p = 1
D vs. C	.747	2	p = .688

Error rates were also analyzed with a linear mixed-effects model (Model A) by using the lme4 package in R (Bates et al., 2014) where Prime (Tone 2, Tone 3, Control) and Frequency (log-transformed word frequencies of Mandarin tone 3 sandhi targets) were considered as fixed variables, and subject as well as item were regarded as random variables. The results of this model revealed that neither the Tone 3 condition yielded significantly lower error rates when compared to the Control condition, $z(987) = 1.291$, $p = .197$, nor the Tone 2 condition produced significantly different error rates from the Control condition, $z(987) = -.501$, $p = .616$. Furthermore, there was no main effect of Frequency either ($z(987) = 1.452$, $p = .147$), showing that word frequency was not a factor for the error data. The lack of the Prime and Frequency effects could be due to overall low error rates across tone 3 sandhi targets. In order to further examine the contribution of First syllable frequency, Second syllable frequency, as well as Prime X Frequency interaction to participants' error rates, a set of follow-up likelihood ratio tests was conducted, as shown in Table 2. Results revealed that First syllable frequency (Model B vs. Model A), Second syllable frequency (Model C vs. Model B), and Prime X Frequency interaction (Model D vs. Model C) were not significant factors in influencing participants' error rates, indicating that the more complex models failed to explain more variance in the error rate data. Although the error rate results here were not fully consistent with those yielded by the ANOVA analyses (significant main effect of Frequency), the linear mixed-effects model for the error data showed no differences. Both analyses revealed no significant speed accuracy trade-offs.

Table 2 Error Rate Likelihood Ratio Tests: Model Comparisons

Model	Factor 1	Factor 2	Factor 3	Factor 4	Factor 5
A	Prime	Freq	N/A	N/A	N/A
B	Prime	Freq	FSFreq	N/A	N/A
C	Prime	Freq	FSFreq	SSFreq	N/A
D	Prime	Freq	FSFreq	SSFreq	Prime X Freq

Model Comparison	χ^2	Df	p value
B vs. A	.614	1	$p = .433$
C vs. B	.088	1	$p = .767$
D vs. C	4.449	2	$p = .108$

2.5 Discussion

This study was designed to investigate how Mandarin tone 3 sandhi words are represented in the native speakers' mental lexicon. The reaction time results of this study showed that Mandarin tone 3 sandhi targets preceded by monosyllabic tone 3 primes elicited significantly faster reaction times than those preceded by both monosyllabic tone 2 primes and control primes. Our data for the facilitation effect, that is, subtracting the reaction times in the Tone 2 and Tone 3 conditions from those in the baseline Control condition, further demonstrated that Mandarin monosyllabic tone 3 primes significantly facilitated participants' lexical decision responses to the following Mandarin tone 3 sandhi targets, whereas Mandarin monosyllabic tone 2 primes failed to facilitate participants' responses to the following Mandarin tone 3 sandhi targets. With regard to the error analyses, our data were consistent with the reaction time analyses and illustrated that subjects made slightly fewer errors, particularly for the low frequency stimuli, when Mandarin tone 3 sandhi targets were preceded by monosyllabic tone 3 primes as compared to when they were preceded by monosyllabic tone 2 primes. These results indicate that tone 3 primes did result in priming while tone 2 primes did not. These data suggest that although tone 3 primes and the first syllable of their corresponding tone 3 sandhi targets did not share the same surface tones, their underlying tonal overlap did facilitate subjects' lexical decisions. Moreover, even when those monosyllabic tone 2 primes and their corresponding tone 3 sandhi targets were entirely matched on their first syllables on the surface, the surface tone 2 overlap did not facilitate subjects' responses when judging the following Mandarin tone 3 sandhi targets. As a result, our data support the canonical representation view in which subjects access the underlying representations /tone 3 tone 3/ and reject the surface representation view in which subjects access the surface representations [tone 2 tone 3]. Mandarin native speakers seem to represent tone 3 sandhi words as /tone 3 tone 3/ in the mental lexicon. The surface representations ([tone 2 tone 3]) of the tone 3 sandhi words do not contribute much to the lexical access of Mandarin tone 3 sandhi words. Rather, Mandarin speakers seem to access the underlying tone 3 of the first syllables of the tone 3 sandhi words in order to recognize them.

Our data are not compatible with the claim in the first experiment in Zhou and Marslen-Wilson (1997), supporting a surface representation view (tone 3 sandhi words represented as /tone 2 tone 3/). The results of the current study show that tone 3 monosyllabic primes facilitated subjects' reaction times in the lexical decision task, showing significantly faster reaction times in the Tone 3 condition than in the Tone 2 condition. The unrelated Control condition in this study served as the baseline in the lexical decision task, with a facilitation effect evident in the Tone 3 condition and no facilitation in the Tone 2 condition. These data are not fully consistent with the explanation of the data in the first experiment in Zhou and Marslen-Wilson (1997) in the sense that they obtained an inhibition effect when tone 3 sandhi targets were preceded by disyllabic primes beginning with a tone 2 syllable and a facilitation effect when the targets were preceded by disyllabic primes starting with a tone 3 syllable. Zhou and Marslen-Wilson (1997) suggested that the disyllabic tone 2 primes slowed down subjects' reaction times of the lexical decision to the tone 3 sandhi targets because of cohort competition at the word level, and the disyllabic tone 3 primes facilitated them thanks to the morphological facilitation at the morpheme level. In their first experiment, since they proposed that the surface tone 2 of the first syllable of the tone 3 sandhi words should be stored directly in the underlying representation (based on the surface representation view), there would be no cohort competition in their tone 3 condition, and a competition effect in the tone 2 condition.

However, as already noted in Zhou and Marslen-Wilson (1997), the same pattern of results could be observed under the canonical representation view if subjects adopted strategic processing. In this scenario, it is possible that their subjects would be biased towards a tone 2 interpretation for the first syllable of the tone 3 sandhi targets simply because there were just too many tone 2 syllables in the stimulus set. A tone 2 bias for the interpretation of the first syllable of the Mandarin tone 3 sandhi words is not beneficiary but harmful under the canonical representation view (UR: /tone 3 tone 3/) since subjects need to access the underlying tone 3 in order to recognize them. The biased tone 2 interpretation would definitely slow down the lexical access of those sandhi words. For their tone 3 condition, their results can be explained under the canonical representation view simply based on the underlying tone 3 overlap between the first syllables of the primes and tone 3 sandhi targets (morpheme level facilitation), without cohort competition on the word level being involved.

The data in the first experiment of Zhou and Marslen-Wilson (1997) were, in fact, consistent with those in Zhou and Marslen-Wilson (1995) where disyllabic targets preceded by disyllabic targets yielded a facilitation effect if the first syllable of the primes and the first syllable of the targets shared the same morpheme (morphological condition), but an inhibition effect if they were homophonous (homophone condition). The morphological condition in Zhou and Marslen-Wilson (1995) was comparable to the tone 3 prime condition in Zhou and Marslen-Wilson (1997) in which primes and tone 3 sandhi targets shared the same first syllable both on the segmental level and tonal level in the underlying representation. The spread of activation from the first syllable of the tone 3 sandhi targets to the whole words after hearing the first syllable of the primes resulted in the facilitation effect. The homophone condition in Zhou and Marslen-Wilson (1995) was similar to the tone 2 prime condition in Zhou and Marslen-Wilson (1997) where the first syllable of the primes and the first syllable of the tone 3 sandhi targets were matched on the segmental and tonal levels on the surface. Cohort competition between primes and tone 3 sandhi targets on the word level led to the inhibition effect. Therefore, the data in Zhou and Marslen-Wilson (1997) can also be fully explained under the canonical representation view.

Our data pattern similarly to the data in the first experiment of Zhou and Marslen-Wilson (1997). Although their primes were all disyllabic words while ours were monosyllabic words, the tone 3 primes in both Zhou and Marslen-Wilson (1997) and the current study elicited significantly stronger facilitation effects than did the tone 2 primes. What is unique in the current study is the lack of cohort competition at the word level (no inhibition effect). Since Mandarin monosyllabic content words are not frequently used, it is very likely that the monosyllabic tone 3 primes, which were all content words in the present study, activated their corresponding tone 3 monosyllabic homophones only on the morpheme level, one of which was the one used as the first morpheme of the tone 3 sandhi targets. The spread of activation of the pre-activated tone 3 morpheme (morpheme level) to the entire tone 3 sandhi targets (word level) after subjects heard them resulted in facilitation, rather than the inhibition triggered by cohort competition on the word level. That may be the reason why there is no inhibition effect in the current study even for the Tone 2 condition. Moreover, since the monosyllabic tone 2 primes did not trigger any morphemes used in the targets, there was no facilitation effect in the Tone 2 condition either.

As for the second experiment in Zhou and Marslen-Wilson (1997), the authors stated that their results were not compatible with either the surface representation view or the canonical representation view. It is worth noting that their tone 2 and tone 3 sandhi conditions patterned similarly, producing a similar degree of inhibition to the tone 2 disyllabic targets. Nevertheless, the tone 3 and tone 3 sandhi conditions differed significantly, with the tone 3 condition eliciting stronger inhibition. One possibility for the pattern of results in their second experiment could be that the primes in the tone 2 and the tone 3 sandhi conditions were matched on their tones on the surface ([tone 2 tone 3]), whereas the tones of the primes in the tone 3 condition ([tone 3 tone 2]) were different. Due to the identical tonal combination for the primes in the tone 2 and the tone 3 sandhi conditions, subjects might have been biased towards the [tone 2 tone 3] interpretation even when encountering tone 3 sandhi primes.

The identical tonal interpretation in the tone 2 and tone 3 sandhi conditions might be the reason why the inhibition effects in these two conditions did not differ. The stronger inhibition effect in the tone 3 condition might be because the first tone 3 syllable of the primes in the tone 3 condition biased the participants' interpretation of the first syllable of the targets towards tone 3, which was not true, resulting in processing burden, thus, stronger inhibition.

The facilitation effect in the current study for both tone prime conditions (primes and the first syllable of the target shared the same segments) is also compatible with the data pattern in Sereno and Lee (2015) where a facilitation effect was shown in the S condition (the prime and the target were matched on segments but not on tones). Although the primes were monosyllabic and the targets were disyllabic in the present study, which is different from the monosyllabic primes and monosyllabic targets used in Sereno and Lee (2015), the current data still show that segmental overlap between primes and targets facilitated subjects' reaction times.

In addition to the perception data showing how Mandarin tone 3 sandhi words are processed, production data also show evidence that Mandarin speakers have some knowledge of the Mandarin tone 3 sandhi rule, which can be used to derive a surface tone 2 syllable from a tone 3 syllable when it is followed by another tone 3 syllable. In Zhang and Lai (2010), for example, Mandarin speakers were asked to combine two tone 3 monosyllables together and produce them as a disyllabic word. The F0 height and contour of the first syllable of the disyllabic stimuli were then analyzed. Five types of stimuli were examined, i.e., AO-AO (i.e., real tone 3 sandhi words; AO = actual occurring morpheme), *AO-AO (i.e., both syllables were actual occurring morphemes, but the combination of the two was a nonword), AO-AG (i.e., the second syllable was an accidental gap [AG], which is a legal combination of Mandarin segments and tones, but only accidentally non-existing), AG-AO (i.e., the first syllable was an accidental gap; the second syllable was an actual occurring morpheme), and AG-AG (i.e., both syllables were accidental gaps). Results showed that Mandarin tone 3 sandhi applied to all types of stimuli 100 percent of the time, with the first syllable of the stimuli, regardless of stimulus type, changed from a low tone (tone 3) to a high rising tone (tone 2). Such a high application rate for Mandarin tone 3 sandhi might be because Mandarin tone 3 sandhi has both phonetic and phonotactic motivations. The phonetic motivation for Mandarin tone 3 sandhi lies in the fact that a shorter tone is preferred in the non-phrasal final position since this position tends to be reduced in duration. Tone 3 (/214/) is the longest tone of the four tones in Mandarin. Changing the longest tone to a shorter tone in the non-phrasal final position, therefore, is phonetically motivated. Moreover, Mandarin does not allow two tone 3 syllables to occur together, so that the first tone 3 syllable has to be changed to a tone 2 syllable. Given that the first tone 3 syllable was successfully changed to a tone 2 syllable across all stimulus types (even for accidental gaps) when followed by another tone 3 syllable in Zhang and Lai (2010), Mandarin speakers showed sensitivity to the tone 3 sandhi rule, applying it even to nonwords. It is likely that Mandarin speakers represent the sandhi stimuli as /tone 3 tone 3/ in their mental lexicon. The surface representation [tone 2 tone 3] of tone 3 sandhi words seems to be derived from the underlying representation /tone 2 tone 2/ via the tone 3 sandhi rule.

The results of the tone effects in this study are also compatible with those of Politzer-Ahles and Zhang (2014), who used the odd-man-out implicit priming paradigm to investigate the effect of tonal representation on production. In implicit priming, a set of words are produced faster when they are phonologically homogeneous than when they are phonologically heterogeneous. In their experiments, four sets of disyllabic words were created, each containing four words. Three of the four words were identical and began with a tone 2 syllable (e.g., tu2-di4), whereas the fourth word in each set was either a completely unrelated word (Unrelated) (e.g., ju4-ti3), a word sharing the same first syllable as the other three words (Homogeneous) (e.g., tu2-mo3), a word beginning with a tone 3 syllable (Heterogeneous) (tu3-dou4), or a word beginning with a sandhi-derived tone 2 syllable (Sandhi) (tu3-rang3). Subjects' speech production latencies to the three words shared by conditions were analyzed. Results showed facilitation effects for the Homogeneous set and the Sandhi set relative to the Unrelated baseline. The Homogeneous set elicited significantly faster reaction times than the Sandhi set, whereas the Sandhi set did not significantly differ from the Heterogeneous set. According to the reduced priming effect for the Sandhi set, Politzer-Ahles and Zhang (2014) proposed that although the tone sandhi rule is applied before articulatory encoding happens, there still seems to be some trace of the underlying representation during speech production. The results of the current study similarly revealed that the underlying representations of Mandarin tone 3 sandhi words do matter during lexical access even though the methodologies used in these two studies are quite different.

Previous studies concerning Dutch also provide evidence supporting that it is the underlying representations rather than the surface representations that play a more important role during online processing (Lahiri, Jongman, & Sereno, 1990; Jongman et al., 1992), which is consistent with the present results. Jongman, Sereno, Raaijmakers, and Lahiri (1992) used the characteristics of Dutch where both vowel length and final obstruent voicing are contrastive underlyingly. However, the final obstruents are neutralized on the surface in syllable-final position. Therefore, vowel length becomes the only cue to distinguish /zat/ ([zat], "drunk") from /zaːd/ ([zaːt], seed) on the surface. In their experiment, a vowel length continuum, [at] to [aːt], was created and attached to syllable onset consonants to form two pairs of real words. Words in each pair differed by vowel length and obstruent final voicing underlyingly, such as /zat/-/zaːd/ and /stad/ ([stat], city) - /staːt/ ([staːt], state). An auditory vowel identification task was conducted where subjects were asked to identify the vowel length that they heard in a word and the category boundary between the /a/-/aː/ in both /zat/-/zaːd/ and /stad/-/staːt/ pairs were compared. The results showed that when encountering an ambiguous [a], listeners identify the slightly longer [a] as an underlying /aː/ in the /zat/-/zaːd/ pair, whereas listeners would identify the same vowel as an underlying /a/ in the /stad/-/staːt/ pair because they considered the slightly lengthened [a] to be due to the following underlying voiced obstruent. Based on the results, Jongman, Sereno, Raaijmakers, and Lahiri (1992) concluded that the categorization of the ambiguous vowel in Dutch is influenced by the underlying representation of the following syllable-final obstruent. Hearing the same acoustic continua, listeners' perceptual boundary of /a/-/aː/ was shifted depending on the underlying phonological representation of the vowel's following obstruent. They proposed that the underlying representation is used by listeners online in speech perception and spoken word recognition. This study sheds light on the role of the underlying representation during online speech perception and shows results consistent with the current study, suggesting that the underlying representation in cases of phonological alternations is of paramount importance, both segmentally and suprasegmentally.

With regard to the frequency effect, the present results showed that overall high frequency tone 3 sandhi targets elicited significantly faster reaction times than did low frequency tone 3 sandhi targets. The reaction times increased as word frequency decreased, showing an expected negative correlation, with faster reaction times for higher frequency targets. The first syllable and second syllable frequency analyses showed no effect between syllable frequencies and reaction times, indicating that subjects' reaction times in the lexical decision task were mainly driven by the word frequency of the tone 3 sandhi compounds, rather than the individual syllable frequencies. The results are also consistent with Zhou and Marslen-Wilson (1994), which investigated the representation of Mandarin disyllabic compounds in the Mandarin speakers' mental lexicon where the first-syllable-frequency effect for Mandarin disyllabic compounds only showed up when the word frequency, morpheme frequency and the second syllable frequency were all held constant. Both the present study and Zhou and Marslen-Wilson (1994) showed that disyllabic word frequency is a dominant factor in influencing subjects' reaction times in Mandarin. Nonetheless, the reduced priming effect in the morphological condition and the null effect in the homophone and character conditions observed in Zhou and Marslen-Wilson (1995) demonstrated an interaction between morpheme-level facilitation and word-level competition in Mandarin.

In the present study, the Prime X Frequency interaction effect did not reach significance, indicating that tone 3 primes did not consistently facilitate subjects' reaction times to a greater extent than did tone 2 primes across the two different frequency groups. The results did not conform to our predictions, which stated that tone 2 primes would either elicit faster or slower reaction times than tone 3 primes for higher frequency tone 3 sandhi targets and tone 3 primes would yield faster or slower reaction times than tone 2 primes for lower frequency tone 3 sandhi targets. The present data show that Mandarin tone 3 sandhi words, regardless of word frequency, are represented as /tone 3 tone 3/ in the native speakers' mental lexicon and their underlying representations, rather than their surface representations, are accessed during online lexical processing. These data support the canonical representation view and oppose the surface representation view. The fact that the tone 3 primes in this study primed the tone 3 sandhi targets even though their surface representations were not matched (tone 3) suggests that Mandarin native speakers *do* process tone 3 sandhi words computationally, making phonological inferences for the first tone 2 syllable on the surface, based on whether or not the second syllable is a tone 3. If it is, then the first tone 2 syllable is evaluated as a tone 3 syllable underlyingly.

The facilitation effects observed in the current study cannot be explained by strategic processing used by subjects in the lexical decision task. Previous studies using phonological overlap with non-tone languages have found priming effects with primes and targets matched on rimes or syllable-initial morphemes (Burton et al., 1996; Slowiaczek et al., 2000; Hamburger & Slowiaczek, 1996; Radeau et al., 1995; McQueen & Sereno, 2005). The effects can be due to both automatic processing and strategic processing, moderated by relatedness proportion, task, and ISI (inter-stimulus interval). In terms of the facilitation effect observed in the current study, it is most likely attributed to automatic processing matching between monosyllabic primes and the first syllables of the disyllabic targets during lexical access rather than strategic processing. It was the tone 3 prime condition that produced much stronger facilitation effect than the tone 2 prime, with matching occurring underlyingly. In addition, McQueen and Sereno (2005) proposed that strategic processing would most likely occur at long ISIs (longer than

500 ms in their study), while automatic processing would be observed at short ISIs. Given the 250 ms ISI used in the present study, it would be more difficult for the subjects to develop strategies when doing the lexical decision task. Furthermore, our fillers balanced the distribution of tones across conditions, which made it more difficult for the subjects to expect what would come next for the target given the specific prime that they had heard. As a result, the facilitation effect obtained in the tone 3 prime condition seems to be due to the influential role of the underlying representation of the tone 3 sandhi words, not because of strategies adopted by subjects during the task.

2.6 Conclusion

The current study investigated how Mandarin tone 3 sandhi words are represented in the native speakers' mental lexicon, testing the validity of the surface representation view and the canonical representation view. Our data showed faster reaction times, lower error rates, and a stronger facilitation effect in the Tone 3 condition than in the Tone 2 condition, regardless of word frequency. These data indicate that Mandarin tone 3 sandhi words are represented as /tone 3 tone 3/ and this representation is accessed during online processing by Mandarin speakers. This /tone 3 tone 3/ representation is used not only for higher frequency tone 3 sandhi words, but also for lower frequency tone 3 sandhi words.

Chapter 3
Priming the Representation of Southern Min Tone Sandhi Words

3.0 Introduction

Chien, Sereno, and Zhang (2016) (based on Chapter 2 of this book) investigated how Mandarin tone 3 sandhi words are processed. An auditory-auditory priming lexical decision experiment was conducted where each disyllabic Mandarin tone 3 sandhi target (e.g., /fu3 dao3/ 辅导, "to counsel") was preceded by one of the three corresponding monosyllabic primes, namely, a tone 2 prime (e.g., /fu2/ 服, "to assist"), a tone 3 prime (e.g., /fu3/ 辅, "to guide"), and a control prime (always a tone 1) (e.g., /fu1/ 敷, to put on). Results showed that tone 3 primes (underlying form overlap with the first syllable of the tone 3 sandhi targets) facilitated participants' lexical decision responses, but tone 2 primes (surface form overlap with the first syllable of the tone 3 sandhi targets) did not relative to the unrelated control primes, regardless of targets' word frequency. These results indicated that tone 3 primes facilitated reaction times due to morpheme-level activation between primes and the first syllable of targets, while tone 2 primes failed to trigger cohort competition at the word level due to the uneven number of syllables between primes (monosyllabic) and targets (disyllabic), giving rise to the null result. Chien, Sereno, and Zhang (2016) concluded that Mandarin tone 3 sandhi words may be represented as /tone 3 tone 3/ at some level of spoken word recognition and word frequency is not a factor in how these words are processed in Mandarin.

Tone sandhi in Southern Min dialect is more complex. It is right-dominant, in that the tone at the right edge of a tone sandhi domain maintains its citation tone (see Table 3 for Southern Min tonal inventory), while the others in the same domain undergo tone sandhi (Lin, 1994). For Southern Min disyllabic words, tone sandhi is manifested in a circular chain-shift fashion in the non-phrasal final position for open syllables or syllables ending with a nasal coda, as shown in Figure 9. Take the syllable 马 /ma51/ as an example. The citation tone of the syllable 马 /ma51/ "horse" changes from a high-falling tone to a high-level tone [ma55] when it precedes another syllable 上 /sjoŋ33/ "above". Thus, the surface form of this Southern Min disyllabic sandhi word 马上 /ma51 sjoŋ33/ "immediately" is [ma55 sjoŋ33].

Table 3 Southern Min Tones

Tone Type	Long tone				Short tone	
Notation	55	24	33	21	51	4	32

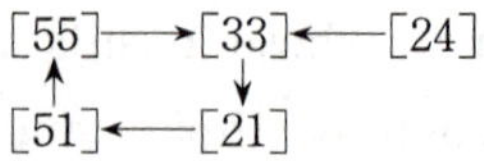

[55]⟶[33]⟵[24]
[51]⟵[21]

Figure 9 Southern Min Tone Sandhi Circle (for Long Tones)

To our knowledge, few priming studies have been conducted to investigate how Southern Min tone sandhi words are represented and processed online. Recent studies on the productivity of Southern Min tone sandhi have demonstrated that the productivity of a particular tone sandhi pattern in Southern Min dialect is influenced by various factors, including opacity of Southern Min tone sandhi and phonotactic motivation (Zhang & Lai, 2008; Zhang, Lai, & Sailor, 2011). Zhang, Lai, and Sailor (2011) tested Southern Min tone sandhi productivity by asking native speakers to reduplicate real words with Actual Occurring reduplication (AO group), real words with no Actual Occurring reduplication (*AO group), and Accidental Gaps (AG group). Their results showed that Southern Min tone sandhi, different from Mandarin tone 3 sandhi, was not particularly productive especially for nonwords. More specifically, tone 51 → tone 55 yielded only around 70 percent correct application for the AO group, 60 percent for the *AO group, and less than 40 percent for the AG group, indicating that unlike Mandarin tone 3 sandhi, Southern Min tone sandhi 51 → 55 was not very productive even for real tone sandhi words. In contrast, Southern Min tone sandhi 24 → 33 was much more productive, eliciting almost 100 percent application for AO and *AO groups, and about 80 percent for the AG group.

Zhang, Lai, and Sailor (2011) suggested that the lower productivity for Southern Min tone sandhi than for Mandarin tone 3 sandhi might be due to the opaque nature of Southern Min tone sandhi (a circular chain shift). Zhang, Lai, and Sailor (2011) further suggested that the reason why tone 51 → tone 55 is relatively less productive compared to tone 24 → tone 33 is possibly due to its lack of phonotactic motivation. It is phonotactically valid for tone 51 to occur in the non-phrase-final position in Southern Min dialect because tone 21 changes to tone 51 in this position. Changing tone 51 to tone 55 in the non-phrase-final position, thus, is not phonotactically motivated, leading to lower productivity. In contrast, it is phonotactically illegal for tone 24 to occur in the non-phrase-final position in Southern Min dialect (see Figure 9). Such phonotactic violation forces tone 24 to undergo tone sandhi, changing to tone 33 in the non-phrase final position. Hence, tone 24 → tone 33 is phonotactically motivated, resulting in higher productivity.

The results in Zhang, Lai, and Sailor (2011) showed that the opaque nature of Southern Min tone sandhi and phonotactic motivation *do* influence Southern Min speakers' sensitivity to Southern Min tone sandhi rules. The relatively unproductive nature of Southern Min tone sandhi in nonwords and even in real words suggested that Southern Min speakers might be less sensitive to Southern Min tone sandhi rules compared with Mandarin speakers to the Mandarin tone 3 sandhi rule. It is likely that Southern Min speakers store the surface representations of tone sandhi words directly in their mental lexicon rather than derive their surface forms from their underlying representations. Furthermore, different degrees of productivity between Southern Min tone sandhi 51 → 55 and 24 → 33 may result from phonotactic motivation, suggesting that the presence or absence of phonotactic motivation might further impact Southern Min speakers' sensitivity to the two representations of Southern Min tone sandhi words.

Based on the previous priming studies on Mandarin tone 3

sandhi and productivity studies on Mandarin and Southern Min tone sandhi, four hypotheses were proposed. First, although Southern Min tone sandhi 51 → 55 and 24 → 33 were not equally productive, and various factors such as opacity and phonotactic motivation have been suggested to influence Southern Min tone sandhi application in the productivity studies (Zhang et al., 2008, 2011), the underlying representation might still play a main role in lexical access in perception. If this hypothesis were supported, the underlying condition would elicit the fastest reaction times among the three conditions, which would be compatible with the Mandarin tone sandhi results in Chien et al. (2016). Second, Southern Min tone sandhi words might be processed mainly based on the surface representation. The underlying representation would only play a minor role due to the opaque nature of Southern Min tone sandhi. In this case, surface primes would yield significantly faster reaction times than would underlying primes when compared to the controls. Third, tone sandhi processing might be related to how sensitive Southern Min speakers are to tone sandhi rules. Such sensitivity was embodied by different tone sandhi productivity, suggested to be impacted by opacity and phonotactic motivation. Hence, not only would Mandarin tone 3 sandhi processing be different from Southern Min tone sandhi, but Southern Min tone sandhi 51 → 55 and tone sandhi 24 → 33 would be processed differently as well. If this hypothesis were supported, surface primes and underlying primes would elicit different reaction time patterns for tone sandhi 51 → 55 and 24 → 33. Finally, frequency of occurrence might go hand-in-hand with the relevance of the surface and underlying representations. If the underlying representation contributes more to Southern Min tone sandhi word processing, then we may not expect the facilitation effect to be regulated by frequency (similar to the Mandarin priming results). However, if the surface representation is relevant, we may expect an interaction between frequency and facilitation (underlying priming vs. surface priming).

Taken together, although the Southern Min tone sandhi productivity results in Zhang and Lai (2008) and Zhang et al. (2011) provide evidence for how Southern Min tone sandhi words are processed, additional evidence from perception experiments is still needed, so that we can directly examine how Southern Min tone sandhi words are represented in speakers' mental lexicon, how tone sandhi words are processed, and compare the processing of Southern Min tone sandhi words with that of Mandarin tone 3 sandhi words. This study sheds light on whether the nature of tone sandhi characteristics influences tone sandhi processing and representations within the same language and across different languages.

3.1 The Current Study

The current study investigates how Southern Min native speakers access Southern Min tone sandhi words and whether Southern Min tone sandhi words and Mandarin tone 3 sandhi words are processed differently due to the different degrees of their productivity caused by the transparent/opaque nature of the sandhi patterns. An auditory-auditory priming lexical decision experiment was conducted on tone sandhi 51 → 55 and 24 → 33. These two tone sandhi patterns were chosen since they patterned differently in terms of productivity in the previous literature, which may be because tone sandhi 24 → 33 is phonotactically motivated while tone sandhi 51 → 55 is not. The experiment examined prime-target pairs, with monosyllabic primes and disyllabic tone sandhi targets. Each tone sandhi disyllabic target was preceded by either a surface tone prime, an underlying tone prime, or an unrelated control prime. Facilitation or inhibition effects across the three priming conditions were evaluated for each tone sandhi (51 → 55, 24 → 33). Finally, we discuss Southern Min tone sandhi processing as compared to Mandarin tone 3 sandhi processing for a better understanding of the role of tone sandhi characteristics in lexical access.

3.2 Methods

3.2.1 Participants

Thirty-six native Southern Min speakers (19 M; 17 F) participated (ranging from 30-55 years old). None of them had any reported language learning impairments.

3.2.2 Stimuli

Thirty-six disyllabic Southern Min tone sandhi words were selected from an online Southern Min dictionary entitled "闽南语常用词辞典" (http://twblg.dict.edu.tw/holodict_new/default.jsp) as critical targets (see Appendix 3). Eighteen of them had the tonal melody 55-24 (i.e., 51 → 55 in the first syllable), while eighteen of them had the tonal melody 33-51 (i.e., 24 → 33 in the first syllable). Since there is no large Southern Min frequency corpus, a subjective familiarity rating task was also conducted to estimate whether the different sandhi targets were similar in frequency (36 participants rated the stimuli, ranging from 1 ["never heard or said"] to 7 ["very often heard and said"], Flege, Takagi, & Mann, 1996). An independent samples t-test ($t(34) = .221$, $p > .826$) showed no significant difference between the subjective familiarity ratings for the 51 → 55 sandhi targets (X = 5.55, sd = 1.25) compared to the 24 → 33 sandhi targets (X = 5.47, sd = .98).

Each disyllabic target was preceded by one of three monosyllabic primes that shared the same segmental content with the first syllable of the target: a surface tone prime, which is identical to the first syllable in the surface tone, an underlying tone prime, which shares the underlying tone with the first syllable, and an unrelated tone prime with a tone different from both the underlying and surface tones. The three types of monosyllabic primes were all real Southern Min morpheme. Examples of each prime condition for each sandhi target type are shown in Figure 10.

In addition to the 36 critical sandhi targets, 60 disyllabic words (selected from the Taiwanese dictionary and Southern Min Spoken Corpus, Myers & Tsay, 2013) served as filler words (see Appendix 4). Thirty of them were preceded by monosyllabic primes whose segments matched the first syllables of the disyllables, and 30 of them by monosyllabic primes sharing neither segments nor tones with the first syllables of the disyllables. They all

51 → 55 sandhi:

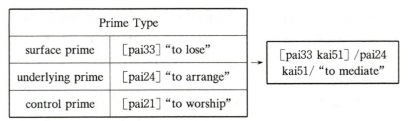

24 → 33 sandhi:

Figure 10 For Each Sandhi Target Type (51 → 55; 24 → 33), There Are Three Prime Conditions

consisted of smooth syllables (open syllables or syllables with a nasal coda). Ninety-six disyllabic nonword targets were also included (see Appendix 4). Each nonword was also preceded by a Southern Min monosyllabic word: 12 were preceded by primes having the same segments and tones as their first syllables, 54 by primes sharing only the same segments with the first syllables, and 30 by primes sharing neither segments nor tones with the first syllables. The numbers of tones were balanced across critical targets, filler words, and nonwords.

3.2.3 Stimulus Recording

A 29-year-old female native Southern Min speaker, without any reported history of language impairments, recorded the stimuli in an anechoic chamber at the University of Kansas with a cardioid microphone (Electrovoice, model N/D767a) and a digital solid-state recorder (Marantz, model PMD671), using a sampling rate of 22,050 Hz.

3.2.4 Procedure

An auditory-auditory priming lexical decision experiment was conducted. For the lexical decision task, stimuli were presented randomly via Paradigm (Tagliaferri, 2015) over headphones (Beats Executive Over-Ear Headphones). Eight practice trials were presented first and then the 192 main trials. For the 192 main trials, 36 of them were critical trials and presented using a Latin Square design, such that each participant only heard a critical target once, preceded by its corresponding surface tone prime, underlying tone prime, or unrelated control prime. The remaining 156 trials were shared across all participants.

For each trial, participants first heard the monosyllabic prime. After a 250 ms interval, they heard the disyllabic target, either a word or a nonword. The participants' task was to judge whether the disyllabic target was a real word or not by clicking the left button of the mouse, representing "yes", or the right button of the mouse, representing "no", as quickly and accurately as possible. The ITI was 3,000 ms. The total duration of the experiment was around 30 minutes. Reaction times and errors obtained from the lexical decision task were subjected to statistical analyses.

3.3 Results

Statistical analyses were conducted on reaction times and

errors obtained from the lexical decision task. The overall error rate was 12.9% (SD = 1.9) (892 trials/6,912 trials). For the reaction time analyses on the critcal targets, incorrect responses (8.8%) and responses over two SDs (3.0%) were excluded.

A series of linear mixed-effects analyses were conducted on participants' log-transformed reaction times and errors using the lme4 package in R (Bates et al., 2014). Likelihood ratio tests were performed to evaluate effects of Prime (Surface, Underlying, Control), Sandhi Type (51 → 55, 24 → 33), Familiarity, Prime X Sandhi Type, Prime X Familiarity, Sandhi Type X Familiarity, and Prime X Sandhi Type X Familiarity.

Participants' log-transformed reaction time to the sandhi targets was set as a dependent variable. Prime and Sandhi Type were categorical independent variables, while Familiarity was a continuous independent variable. For Prime, Control was selected as the baseline to which Surface and Underlying were compared in order to examine facilitation and inhibition effects. Participant and Item were considered random variables. Seven models (A, B, C, D, E, F, and G) were created and compared to determine main effects, as shown in Table 4.

Table 4 Reaction Time Likelihood Ratio Tests: Model Comparisons

Model	Factor 1	Factor 2	Factor 3	Factor 4	Factor 5	Factor 6	Factor 7
A	Prime	N/A	N/A	N/A	N/A	N/A	N/A
B	Prime	Sandhi Type	N/A	N/A	N/A	N/A	N/A
C	Prime	Sandhi Type	Familiarity	N/A	N/A	N/A	N/A

continued

Model	Factor 1	Factor 2	Factor 3	Factor 4	Factor 5	Factor 6	Factor 7
D	Prime	Sandhi Type	Familiarity	Prime X Sandhi Type	N/A	N/A	N/A
E	Prime	Sandhi Type	Familiarity	Prime X Sandhi Type	Prime X Familiarity	N/A	N/A
F	Prime	Sandhi Type	Familiarity	Prime X Sandhi Type	Prime X Familiarity	Sandhi Type X Familiarity	N/A
G	Prime	Sandhi Type	Familiarity	Prime X Sandhi Type	Prime X Familiarity	Sandhi Type X Familiarity	Prime X Sandhi Type X Familiarity

Model Comparison	$\Delta\chi^2$	df	p value
B vs. A	.709	1	$p = .4$
C vs. B	33.161	1	$p < .001$
D vs. C	12.92	2	$p = .002$
E vs. D	3.275	2	$p = .195$
F vs. E	0	1	$p = 1$
G vs. F	14.338	2	$p < .001$

Results generated from the likelihood ratio tests showed an effect of Familiarity by comparing Model C and Model B ($\Delta\chi^2 = 33.161$, df = 1, $p < .001$), indicating that participants responded to familiar targets significantly faster than to unfamiliar targets. Results also showed an effect of Prime X Sandhi Type by comparing Model D and Model C ($\Delta\chi^2 = 12.92$, df = 2, $p = .002$), and an effect of Prime X Sandhi Type X Familiarity by comparing Model G and Model F ($\Delta\chi^2 = 14.338$, df = 2, $p < .001$). There were no main effects for Sandhi Type, nor any Prime X Familiarity or Sandhi Type X Familiarity interactions. We first split Sandhi Type to further examine the two-way interaction of Prime X Sandhi Type, and then investigated effects underlying the three-way interaction.

Additional linear mixed-effects analyses were conducted to examine the significant Prime X Sandhi Type interaction. Two additional analyses were conducted for targets with tone sandhi 51 → 55 and for targets with tone sandhi 24 → 33. Participants' Log-transformed Reaction Time was set as a dependent variable. Prime was treated categorically as a fixed factor (Surface, Underlying, Control). Participant and Item were set as random variables.

For targets with tone sandhi 51 → 55, Surface tone primes elicited significantly faster reaction times than did Control primes ($\beta = -.030$, SE = .007, $t = -4.45$, $p < .001$), and there was a trend for Underlying tone primes to yield faster reaction times than did the Controls ($\beta = -.011$, SE = .007, $t = -1.66$, $p = .097$) (see Figure 11). Reaction times for the Surface prime condition were also significantly faster than those

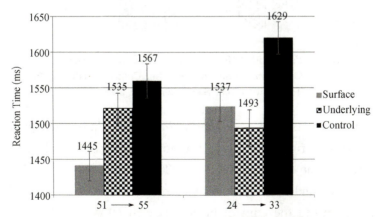

Figure 11　Reaction Times (ms) and Error Bars in the Surface, Underlying, and Control Conditions for Words with Tone Sandhi 51 → 55 and Tone Sandhi 24 → 33

for the Underlying prime condition (β = .020, SE = .007, t = 2.92, p = .004) (see Figure 11). As shown in Figure 12, the facilitation priming revealed that for the targets with tone sandhi 51 → 55, Surface tone primes (+ 120 ms facilitation priming effect) significantly facilitated participants' lexical decision responses. While Underlying tone primes (+ 32 ms facilitation priming effect) showed significantly less facilitation than Surface tone primes, a facilitation effect (relative to Control primes) was still evident.

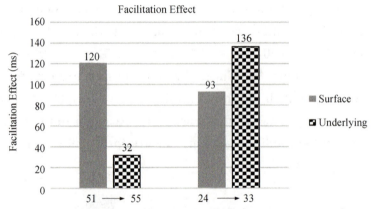

Figure 12 Facilitation Effects for the Surface and Underlying Prime Conditions (Relative to Baseline Control Condition) for Targets with Tone Sandhi 51 → 55 and 24 → 33

For targets with tone sandhi 24 → 33, Underlying primes elicited significantly faster reaction times compared to the Control prime condition (β = − .036, SE = .006, t = − 5.68, p < .001) and Surface primes yielded significantly faster reaction times than did the control primes as well (β = − .023, SE = .006, t = − 3.65, p < .001) (see Figure 11). Furthermore, the Underlying condition elicited significantly faster reaction times than did the Surface condition ($\beta = -.013$, SE = .006, $t = -2.07$, $p = .039$) (see Figure 11). As shown in Figure 12, for targets with tone sandhi 24 → 33, both Underlying and Surface prime conditions significantly facilitated participants' lexical decision responses; however, the facilitation effect yielded by the Underlying condition (+136 ms facilitation priming effect) was significantly stronger than that observed in the Surface condition (+93 ms facilitation priming effect), reversed from what was found for tone sandhi 51 → 55.

To further examine the effect underlying the three-way interaction of Prime X Sandhi Type X Familiarity, two series of likelihood ratio tests were also conducted on participants' log-transformed reaction times within tone sandhi 51 → 55 (Models H, I, and J) (see Table 5) and 24 → 33 (Models K, L, and M) (see Table 6) respectively. Prime (Surface, Underlying, Control) and Familiarity (continuous) were treated as independent variables. Participant and Item were set as random variables. For sandhi 51 → 55, Models H, I, and J were created and compared with each other (see Table 5) to examine effects of Prime, Familiarity, as well as Prime X Familiarity, while for sandhi 24 → 33, Models K, L, and M were generated and compared with each other (see Table 6) to evaluate the same effects.

Table 5 Reaction Time Likelihood Ratio Tests for Tone Sandhi 51 → 55: Model Comparisons

Model	Factor 1	Factor 2	Factor 3
H	Prime	N/A	N/A
I	Prime	Familiarity	N/A
J	Prime	Familiarity	Prime X Familiarity

Model Comparison	$\Delta \chi^2$	df	p value
I vs. H	16.84	1	$p < .001$
J vs. I	5.147	2	$p = .076$

Table 6 Reaction Time Likelihood Ratio Tests for Tone Sandhi 24 → 33: Model Comparisons

Model	Factor 1	Factor 2	Factor 3
K	Prime	N/A	N/A
L	Prime	Familiarity	N/A
M	Prime	Familiarity	Prime X Familiarity

Model Comparison	$\Delta \chi^2$	df	p value
L vs. K	15.491	1	$p < .001$
M vs. L	12.432	2	$p = .002$

Results showed an effect of Familiarity for both tone sandhi 51 → 55 (Model I vs. Model H) and tone sandhi 24 → 33 (Model L vs. Model K), indicating that participants responded to familiar targets significantly faster than to unfamiliar targets regardless of Sandhi Type.

In addition, a significant interaction between Prime and Familiarity was obtained for tone sandhi 24 → 33 (Model M vs. Model L) and a trend for the Prime X Familiarity interaction (Model J vs. Model I) was observed for tone sandhi 51 → 55. Figure 13 below shows the facilitation effects for both Surface and Underlying forms relative to the Control condition for sandhi 51 → 55 and sandhi 24 → 33. The different facilitatory patterns across the two sandhi types confirmed the three-way interaction obtained above, showing significantly different reaction time patterns across Surface and Underlying conditions as a function of Familiarity for words with tone sandhi 51 → 55 compared to words with tone sandhi 24 → 33. As shown in Figure 13, the slope of the surface facilitation is steeper than that for the underlying facilitation, with familiarity affecting the surface form more than that of the underlying form across both sandhi types. Overall, the contribution of the surface and underlying representations depended on the nature of the sandhi characteristics in Southern Min dialect, with familiarity modulating the amount of priming especially for the surface priming effect.

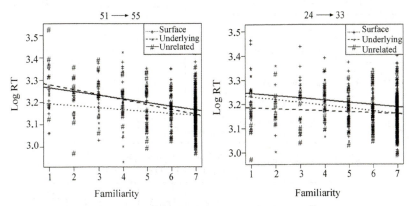

Figure 13 Facilitation Effects for Tone Sandhi 51 → 55 and 24 → 33 as a Function of Familiarity

Linear mixed-effects analyses were also conducted on participants' errors using the lme4 package in R (Bates et al., 2014). A set of likelihood ratio tests were performed to examine main effects of Prime (Surface, Underlying, Control), Sandhi Type (51 → 55, 24 → 33), Familiarity (continuous), Prime X Sandhi Type, Prime X Familiarity, Sandhi Type X Familiarity, and Prime X Sandhi Type X Familiarity. For Prime, Control was chosen as the baseline to which Surface and Underlying were compared. Subject and Item were set as random factors. Models N, O, P, Q, R, S, and T were generated (see Table 7). Results determined Model P to be the best model because models with more variables than Model P could not explain more variance in participants' error data.

Table 7 Error Rate Likelihood Ratio Tests: Model Comparisons

Model	Factor 1	Factor 2	Factor 3	Factor 4	Factor 5	Factor 6	Factor 7
N	Prime	N/A	N/A	N/A	N/A	N/A	N/A
O	Prime	Sandhi Type	N/A	N/A	N/A	N/A	N/A
P	Prime	Sandhi Type	Familiarity	N/A	N/A	N/A	N/A
Q	Prime	Sandhi Type	Familiarity	Prime X Sandhi Type	N/A	N/A	N/A
R	Prime	Sandhi Type	Familiarity	Prime X Sandhi Type	Prime X Familiarity	N/A	N/A
S	Prime	Sandhi Type	Familiarity	Prime X Sandhi Type	Prime X Familiarity	Sandhi Type X Familiarity	N/A
T	Prime	Sandhi Type	Familiarity	Prime X Sandhi Type	Prime X Familiarity	Sandhi Type X Familiarity	Prime X Sandhi Type X Familiarity

Model Comparison	$\Delta \chi^2$	df	p value
O vs. N	.244	1	$p = .621$
P vs. O	49.331	1	$p < .001$
Q vs. P	1.103	2	$p = .576$

continued

Model Comparison	$\Delta\chi^2$	df	p value
R vs. Q	.447	2	$p = .8$
S vs. R	.603	1	$p = .437$
T vs. S	.781	2	$p = .677$

The results from Model P showed that Familiarity is a factor in influencing participants' error rates in the lexical decision task, with less familiar targets eliciting more errors ($\beta = .994$, SE $= .106$, $z = 9.359$, $p < .001$). Moreover, no effect of Prime was observed, indicating that neither the Surface condition ($\beta = -.421$, SE $= .234$, $z = -1.8$, $p = .07$) nor the Underlying condition ($\beta = .061$, SE $= .249$, $z = .244$, $p = .807$) elicited fewer errors than the Control condition and Sandhi Type was not significant either ($\beta = -.133$, SE $= .235$, $z = -.566$, $p = .572$), suggesting a similar number of errors for targets with tone sandhi 51 → 55 and 24 → 33.

3.4 Discussion

The current study investigated how Southern Min speakers represent and process Southern Min words with either tone sandhi 51 → 55 or tone sandhi 24 → 33. A priming methodology was used in which participants heard monosyllabic prime words followed by disyllabic tone sandhi targets. We found significant facilitation effects due to the overlap between the primes and the first syllables of disyllabic tone sandhi targets. Our data show that for targets with tone sandhi 51 → 55 and 24 → 33, both underlying and surface tone primes significantly facilitated participants' lexical decision responses compared to an unrelated control prime condition. Priming occurred when there was overlap either in terms of underlying or surface representation for both tone sandhi conditions.

Significant differences in the nature of the priming across the two Southern Min sandhi types were observed. While both sandhi types exhibited facilitatory priming effects, the contribution of underlying and surface forms across sandhi types was distinct. For targets with tone sandhi 51 → 55, surface tone primes showed significantly more facilitation than underlying tone primes while for targets with tone sandhi 24 → 33, underlying tone primes showed significantly more facilitation than surface tone primes.

Phonotactic constraints of Southern Min tone sandhi may provide an explanation. Zhang, Lai, and Sailor (2011) examined productivity of Southern Min tone sandhi and found measurable differences in productivity across Southern Min tone sandhis. While Southern Min tone sandhi 24 → 33 elicited nearly complete application in the nonce-probe test (80%), tone 51 → tone 55 sandhi yielded only 40% correct application. They argued that tone 24 → tone 33 is more productive compared to tone 51 → tone 55 since it is phonotactically illegal for tone 24 to occur in the non-phrasal final position while it is legal for tone 51 to occur in that position in Southern Min dialect (see Figure 1). These productivity differences in Southern Min tone sandhi were observed in our priming data. For the less productive 51 → 55 sandhi, surface tone primes showed significantly greater priming effects compared to underlying primes while for the more productive tone 24 → tone 33 sandhi, the underlying primes showed significantly greater facilitation effects compared to surface primes. These data suggest that Southern Min words with different tone sandhi characteristics were processed differently depending on differences in phonotactic motivation. For words with the less productive sandhi pattern 51 → 55 (not phonotactically motivated), the surface representation was activated to a greater extent while for words with the more productive sandhi pattern 24 → 33 (phonotactically motivated), the underlying representation played a more crucial role.

These data can be compared to Mandarin tone sandhi, which is very productive and applies without exception to novel disyllable combinations (Zhang & Lai, 2010). Using similar experimental priming methods examining productive Mandarin tone 3 sandhi, only underlying facilitation was observed, with no frequency modulation of the priming effect (Chien, Sereno, & Zhang, 2016).

The present results also showed effects of familiarity on priming. We found familiarity effects that differed across sandhi types. For tone sandhi 51 → 55, familiarity effects emerged with the surface primes yielding most facilitation than the underlying primes when participants were less familiar with the targets. However, for words with tone sandhi 24 → 33, the surface effect increased as familiarity increased, with underlying priming being consistently stronger than surface priming. Comparing these two sandhis, it does appear that the contribution of the surface representation was modulated more by familiarity than that of the underlying representation in Southern Min tone sandhi word processing.

Familiarity or frequency, therefore, only seems to modulate the facilitation effect of surface form primes for sandhi words in Southern Min dialect.

The current priming methodology can be used to observe the representation of tone sandhi words. Participants heard monosyllabic primes followed by disyllabic tone sandhi targets and performed a lexical decision. The facilitation effect is the result of activation between primes and the first syllables of the targets, either in the underlying representation or in the surface representation. No inhibition was observed. These results are also consistent with the results in the first experiment of Zhou and Marslen-Wilson (1997) in which the tone 3 primes (disyllabic) facilitated participants' lexical decision responses due to morpheme level activation between the first syllables of the primes and those of the tone 3 sandhi targets.

The current results are consistent with our hypothesis that Southern Min tone sandhi processing is related to how sensitive Southern Min speakers are to the tone sandhi rules. Such sensitivity is embodied by different patterns for different types of tone sandhi productivity. The current priming studies together show a relationship between productivity and priming, instantiated in a gradient fashion in that the exceptionless, very productive Mandarin tone 3 sandhi only elicited significant underlying facilitation, the slightly less productive Southern Min tone sandhi 24 → 33 produced mostly underlying priming, with surface facilitation being significantly weaker, and the least productive Southern Min tone sandhi 51 → 55 yielded significant surface facilitation, with the underlying representation contributing only little. These findings suggest that words undergoing different sandhi rules across different languages or within the same language are processed and represented differently depending on the characteristics of tone sandhi patterns. These findings shed light on tone sandhi processing at least for languages having the right-dominant sandhi system in which a sandhi tone is usually another lexical tone. More future research has to be conducted to examine how tone sandhi words are processed and represented in languages with a left-dominant tone sandhi system, in which the tone of the left-most syllable is usually spread throughout a whole sandhi domain (Selkirk & Shen, 1990; Chan & Ren, 1989).

The current data can serve as a foundation to unravel issues concerning the nature of the representation of tone sandhi words. Tone sandhi is a phonological process that shows variation in the nature of the lexical representation. For words with productive tone sandhi, speakers are the most sensitive to the underlying representation, and less sensitive to the surface representation. Since the surface representation can be correctly generated by feeding the underlying representation to the tone sandhi computational process, speakers do not have to focus on the surface representation. They can just let the computational process generate correct sandhi forms. The more productive a tone sandhi rule is, the greater the contribution of the underlying representation, suggesting that speakers may represent productive sandhi words in terms of their underlying representations in the mental lexicon. For words with less productive tone sandhi, speakers are more sensitive to the surface representation and less sensitive to the underlying representation. Although speakers can still operate the sandhi rule, since this computational mechanism is not automatic, they still have to store the surface representation. The less productive a tone sandhi is, the greater the contribution of the surface representation. For Southern Min tone sandhi 24 → 33 in which tone 24 goes into the opaque tone sandhi circle, although speakers can apply the sandhi rule and are aware of the underlying representation, they still have to access their surface representations in order to process the words correctly. For Southern Min tone sandhi 51 → 55 which is opaque and not phonotactically motivated, speakers are not sensitive to the sandhi rule. Therefore, they must access their surface representations for word recognition, with the surface representation contributing more and more as familiarity decreases (less and less sensitive to the rule).

3.5 Conclusion

The present study demonstrated that disyllabic Southern Min tone sandhi words are represented differently based on phonotactic constraints. We found significant facilitation effects due to the overlap between the primes and the first syllables of disyllabic tone sandhi targets. Our data show that for targets with tone sandhi 51 → 55 and tone sandhi 24 → 33, both underlying and surface tone primes significantly facilitated participants' lexical decision responses compared to an unrelated control prime condition. The current data can serve to unravel issues concerning the nature of the representation of tone sandhi words. Most interestingly, significant differences in the nature of the priming across the two Southern Min sandhi types were observed. While both sandhi types exhibited facilitatory priming effects, the contribution of underlying and surface forms across sandhi types was different. For targets with tone sandhi 51 → 55, surface tone primes showed significantly more facilitation than underlying tone primes while for targets with tone sandhi 24 → 33, underlying tone primes showed significantly more facilitation than surface tone primes. Moreover, only the surface priming is modulated by frequency for both sandhi types, while the underlying priming is not. The present results clearly demonstrate that words with different tone sandhi characteristics are represented and processed differently in the mental lexicon.

Chapter 4
An ERP Study on Mandarin Tone 3 Sandhi Processing

4.0 Neurophysiological Studies on Lexical Tone Processing

In the past several decades, event-related brain potentials (ERPs) have been used to investigate the neural basis of perception and cognition with extremely high temporal resolution. Although ERPs do not transparently reflect where neural processes occur, they do provide millisecond by millisecond resolution regarding processing stages and neural components linked to perception. One neural component that the speech perception literature has exploited is mismatch negativity. Previous studies have shown that mismatch negativity (MMN) (or mismatch field, MMF, in MEG) reflects deviations from previously presented events or regularities (Näätänen et al., 1997; Kazanina, Phillips, & Idsardi, 2006; Kujala, Tervaniemi, & Schröger, 2007; Phillips et al., 2000; Wang et al., 2012). The MMN is traditionally recorded using an oddball paradigm in which a sequence of similar sounds ("standard") is presented and rare sounds ("deviant") are introduced occasionally. The similar sounds form a memory trace in the auditory system to which deviant sounds contrast, yielding MMN effects around 100 – 250 ms after the onset of deviant sound presentation (Näätänen & Winkler, 1999). The mismatch response has been used to examine the processing of segmental and tonal information in both non-tonal and tone languages, as well as predictive processing in language comprehension. Phillips et al. (2000), for example, used the mismatch response at the segmental level, investigating whether abstract phoneme categories are available at the level of auditory cortex. In their first MEG experiment, physically different [dæ] tokens (varying in VOT) were presented to native English speakers as standards, while physically different [tæ] tokens were presented as deviants. Results showed a mismatch response when participants heard [tæ] tokens, which are phonologically different from [dæ] tokens. The results suggested that English speakers did form phoneme categories for [dæ] tokens and [tæ] tokens and abstracted away from the physical, acoustic differences between the [dæ] tokens and [tæ] tokens. Otherwise, no mismatch response would have been elicited because acoustically speaking, there was not a many-to-one ratio for the stimuli, which is necessary for yielding the mismatch response. In order to make sure that the mismatch response they observed in this study was not because those [dæ] tokens just happened to be physically more similar to each other compared to the [tæ] tokens, a second experiment was conducted in which all [dæ] tokens and [tæ] tokens were increased by 20 ms in terms of their VOTs. The logic here was if it was truly the closer physical distance shared between the [dæ] tokens that drove the results in the first experiment, results would be replicated in the second experiment since the physical distance between stimuli was still the same. However, if it was the participants' phonology that drove the results in the first experiment, no mismatch response would be expected in the second experiment because adding 20 ms VOT corrupted the many-to-one ratio between standards and deviants at the phonological level (i.e., similar numbers of /tæ/ and /dæ/). The results of the second experiment showed no mismatch response, confirming that the results in their first experiment were due to participants' phonology. The data clearly suggest that phonology *does* influence how we categorize and perceive sounds.

With regard to predictive processing in language comprehension, Bendixen, Scharinger, Strauβ & Obleser (2014), for example, sought evidence for it from mismatch responses to omitted speech segments. In their first experiment, German words Lachs ([laks], "salmon") or Latz ([lats], "bib") were presented to German listeners auditorily, with La ([la], no semantic meaning) occasionally mixed in. Results showed significantly stronger omission MMN effects when the context predicted the final segments (only [laks] as the standard vs. [la] as the deviant) than when such prediction was absent (both [laks] and [lats] as standards vs. [la] as the deviant). The results of Bendixen et al. (2014) suggested predictive coding mechanisms in the central auditory system to support spoken word recognition.

With respect to the MMN studies in tone languages, Xi, Zhang, Shu, Zhang, and Li (2010) used MMN to investigate categorical perception between Mandarin lexical tone 2 (/35/)

and tone 4 (/51/). Their results showed that two physically different tones across two distinct tonal categories elicited greater MMN amplitude than did two physically different tones within the same tonal category. Interestingly, physically different tones across tonal categories yielded a stronger MMN amplitude than did physically different tones within the same tonal category in the left hemisphere but not in the right hemisphere. These results suggest that the right-hemisphere may play a more important role for acoustic processing (Xi et al., 2010; Ren, Yang, & Li, 2009), while the left-hemisphere may be more in charge of the long-term phonemic processing of lexical tones (Xi et al., 2010). These data also suggest that acoustic information (right hemisphere) and phonological information (left hemisphere) were processed simultaneously for Mandarin lexical tones in the same MMN time window. Finally, these data demonstrated that non-speech stimuli with the same F0 contours as their corresponding speech counterparts elicited a similar MMN pattern as speech stimuli, indicating that Mandarin speakers can transfer their lexical tone knowledge to non-speech perception (Xi et al., 2010; Ren et al., 2009).

Mismatch negativity has also been shown to be modulated not only by across-or within-category differences between lexical tones, but also by language experience. Chandrasekaran, Krishnan, and Gandour (2007) tested native speakers of Mandarin and English using an odd-ball paradigm in two experimental conditions, namely, a similar tone pair condition (tone 2 vs. tone 3) and a dissimilar tone pair condition (tone 1 vs. tone 3). Results showed that the dissimilar tone pair condition elicited larger MMN amplitude than the similar tone pair condition only for Mandarin speakers. For English speakers, these two conditions yielded comparable MMN amplitudes. Chandrasekaran et al. (2007) suggested that language experience affects early cortical processing of fundamental frequency (F0) contours.

Extracting abstract linguistic rules from varying acoustic signals is of paramount importance in speech perception. This is true for both segmental and tonal processes. Wang et al. (2012) conducted a mismatch negativity study to investigate whether Mandarin speakers possess a sensory mechanism that can help them extract abstract linguistic rules from complicated acoustic information at a pre-attentive stage. Their experiment was conducted using an oddball paradigm in which 90 percent of the monosyllabic stimuli were level tones (standards), carried by different Mandarin vowels (a, e, i, u), with various F0 height (10 levels from 78 Hz to 150 Hz) as well as intensity (3 intensity levels). Only 10 percent of the monosyllabic stimuli were either rising or falling tones (deviants), carried by different Mandarin vowels (a, e, i, u), with three levels of F0 (an identical F0 contour at three different F0 heights) and intensity (same as the three intensities used for the standards). Results showed a mismatch negativity (MMN), indicating that the effect emerged when the pattern formed by level tones was violated. Wang et al. (2012) concluded that there is a pre-attentive sensory intelligence in the perception of Mandarin lexical tones. They suggested that human brains, equipped with this sensory intelligence, can extract linguistically meaningful patterns from complex auditory signals during speech communication without involving attention.

Moving from tone processing in monosyllables to that in disyllables, Gu, Li, Wang, Hou, Huang, and Chen (2012) conducted an event-related potential (ERP) study to examine memory traces for tone language words by manipulating lexicality in an oddball paradigm in which Mandarin monosyllables were used as standards, while deviants were disyllabic. For the deviants, their second syllables, carrying critical tonal information (tone 2 /35/ or tone 4 /51/), made them either a Mandarin word or a nonword. ERP results showed a more negative-going wave when the deviants were real Mandarin disyllabic words compared to when the deviants were disyllabic nonwords. Moreover, this effect peaked at 164 ms after the word recognition point. These results suggest that tonal information can be used online to activate lexical memory traces in tone languages at a very early stage of lexical processing, which is consistent with the time course of the processing of segmental information in non-tonal languages (Gu et al., 2012).

In addition to the studies mentioned above that examine Mandarin tone processing, Li and Chen (2015) conducted a mismatch negativity study to examine Mandarin lexical tone representations involving tonal alternations, especially focusing on tone 3, which alternates with tone 2 when followed by another tone 3. An oddball experiment was conducted in which monosyllable [ma] with tone 1, tone 2, and tone 3 were set as stimuli. Four conditions were generated: T1 standard/T3 deviant, T3 standard/T1 deviant, T2 standard/T3 deviant, and T3 standard/T2 deviant. Results showed that all four conditions elicited MMN effects. However, the patterns of MMN effects were different, with T1 standard/T3 deviant and T3 standard/T1 deviant yielding comparable MMN effects, but T2 standard/T3 deviant and T3 standard/T2 deviant showing asymmetrical MMN effects. When T3 was the standard and T2 was the deviant, the MMN effect was significantly reduced than when T2 was the standard and T3 was the deviant. Moreover, only the MMN elicited in the T3 standard/T2 deviant condition demonstrated a right hemispheric distribution, and all the other three conditions showed a left hemispheric distribution in MMN effects. Based on these results, Li and Chen (2015) proposed that Mandarin tone 3 should be represented as both /tone 3/ and /tone 2/ in the mental lexicon. They claimed that the reduced and right lateralized MMN effect in the T3 standard/T2 deviant condition may be because when participants heard a tone 3 syllable, both tone 3 and tone 2 representations were activated. Thus, the activated tone 2 representation was not in conflict with the deviant tone 2, leading to the reduced and right-hemispheric distributed MMN effect.

Li and Chen's (2015) results provided evidence that Mandarin tone 3 might have two representations, i.e., a low-dipping contour and a high-rising contour given the asymmetric MMN effects observed in the T2 standard/T3 deviant and T3 standard/T2 deviant conditions. It should be noted that these data were found with isolated syllables. For disyllabic contexts, it is still unclear how Mandarin native speakers process the tone of the first syllable of Mandarin tone 3 sandhi words, which acoustically is a tone 2. Whether Mandarin speakers process the initial sandhi tone 2 of tone 3 sandhi words as a tone 2 or a tone 3, or whether speakers assign a special status to the initial sandhi tone 2 and wait for the context (i.e., either a tone 3 syllable or not) is unclear. Given these possibilities, it is warranted to further investigate the representation of Mandarin tone 3 sandhi words at the cortical level.

Zhang, Xia, and Peng (2015) used Mandarin disyllables to investigate the phonological encoding of Mandarin tone 3 sandhi words. A speech production task was conducted during which participants were asked to put two auditorily presented syllables together and pronounce them as a whole chunk covertly as soon as they heard the two syllables (e.g., T2 + T3 and T3 + T3). Participants had to pronounce those disyllables as a unit overtly after a silent interval varying between 1,000 and 1,600 ms. Zhang et al.'s (2015) goal was to test whether Mandarin tone 3 sandhi words undergo either a computation mechanism, which converts the first tone 3 syllable into a tone 2 syllable, or a lexical mechanism, which allows tone 3 sandhi words' surface forms to be directly accessed before being sent to speech production. Notice that tone 3 syllables were always presented as a canonical falling-rising tone [214] rather than as their sandhi form [35]. Hence, participants had to transform the canonical falling-rising tone 3 of the first syllable of a disyllabic sequence into a tone 2 in order to produce the correct output.

Zhang et al. (2015) a found significantly greater P2 amplitude (i.e., a neural component argued to reflect higher-order perceptual processing, modulated by attention, repetition effects and task difficulties (Landi et al., 2012; Dunn et al., 1998; Kim et al., 2008)) at mid-line electrodes elicited by tone 3 syllables preceded by a tone 3 syllable than preceded by a tone 2 syllable. The stronger P2 amplitude yielded by the second tone 3 syllable of Mandarin tone 3 sandhi words indicated that Mandarin speakers did spend additional effort processing and phonologically encoding tone 3 sandhi words. Moreover, no significant P2 difference was observed between real tone 3 sandhi words and tone 3 sandhi nonwords, demonstrating that Mandarin speakers process tone 3 sandhi words computationally, applying the tone 3 sandhi rule even to pseudowords.

However, the greater P2 effect elicited by the tone 3 syllables preceded by other tone 3 syllables could also be because it was easier for the participants to produce words (T2 + T3) that were matched on what they heard (T2 + T3) than to produce words that did not match what they heard (T3 + T3). Additionally, the fact that participants were provided the canonical tone 3 form explicitly might force them to focus on the underlying representation of tone 3 sandhi syllables (falling-rising F0 contour), which might make participants use extra effort to convert what they heard (a falling-rising F0 contour) to what they were going to produce (rising F0 contour).

To sum up, previous studies on tone sandhi *do* provide some suggestive evidence regarding the representation of Mandarin tones and how Mandarin tone 3 sandhi words are processed. For example, Li and Chen (2015) proposed that Mandarin tone 3 (monosyllable) should be represented as both tone 2 and tone 3 in the mental lexicon, and Zhang, Xia and Peng (2015) suggested that Mandarin tone 3 sandhi words should be processed in a computational fashion from a tone 3 before speech production. However, these studies did not explicitly examine how Mandarin speakers process the surface initial tone 2 syllable of disyllabic Mandarin tone 3 sandhi words during spoken word recognition. It is therefore warranted to incorporate electrophysiological approaches to examine the processing of tone sandhi words at a very early stage of language comprehension. Consequently, a mismatch negativity experiment was conducted to examine how Mandarin tone 3 sandhi words are processed at the pre-attentive stage, and test the role of surface and underlying representations of Mandarin tone 3 sandhi words during spoken word recognition. The current study used disyllabic Mandarin tone 3 sandhi words as stimuli and a perception experiment as the method to tackle these issues.

4.1 The Current Mismatch Negativity Experiment

A mismatch negativity experiment was conducted to investigate Mandarin tone 3 sandhi words. This experiment focused on how Mandarin speakers process tone 3 sandhi words at an early stage. The data will provide evidence for the early processing of Mandarin tone 3 sandhi words independent of any overt behavioral response. This method will avoid effects from later processing stages, which might influence reaction times from lexical decision tasks. In the current study, an oddball paradigm was used, in which disyllabic words with an initial tone 2 syllable ([tone 2 tone 4] /tone 2 tone 4/) (Tone 2 Condition), disyllabic words with an initial tone 3 syllable ([tone 3 tone 4] /tone 3 tone 4/) (Tone 3 Condition), and disyllabic tone 3 sandhi words ([tone 2 tone 3] /tone 3 tone 3/) (Sandhi Condition) were included as standards in three different conditions. In a fourth condition, standards consisted of disyllabic tone 3 sandhi words ([tone 2 tone 3] /tone 3 tone 3/) mixed with disyllabic words starting with a tone 3 syllable ([tone 3 tone 4] /tone 3 tone 4/) (Mix Condition). Note that the initial syllables of the standards were matched on segmental information across all conditions. A tone 2 monosyllable was used as deviants in all four conditions, with the same segments as the first syllable of the standards.

Four within condition comparisons were conducted in which ERPs elicited by the deviant and those yielded by the first syllable of standards in the same condition were compared. If we observed that the ERP waveforms elicited by the deviant were significantly more negative than those yielded by the first syllable of standards, then we could claim to have found an MMN effect at the deviant position within each condition. Most importantly, if we obtained an MMN effect at the deviant position in both the Tone 2 Condition and the Sandhi Condition, the result would suggest similar neural mechanisms involved in the processing of the initial tone 2 syllable of both disyllabic Mandarin tone 2 words and tone 3 sandhi words. If we observed an MMN effect only in one of the two conditions, then the result would suggest different neural mechanisms employed between the initial tone 2 syllable of disyllabic

Mandarin tone 2 words and that of Mandarin tone 3 sandhi words.

4.2 Methods

4.2.1 Participants

Twenty right-handed native Mandarin speakers were recruited (8 males and 12 females), aged 18 to 35 at the time of testing. All participants were students from the University of Kansas with no reported language disability or hearing impairment. All participants were asked to provide informed consent before the EEG experiment, and were given 20 US dollars as compensation after the experiment.

4.2.2 Stimuli

Stimuli were produced by a male native Beijing Mandarin speaker and recorded in an anechoic chamber with a cardioid microphone (Electrovoice, model N/D767a) and a digital solid-state recorder (Marantz, model PMD671), using a sampling rate of 22,050 Hz at the University of Kansas. Stimuli used in this experiment were ten disyllabic Mandarin words and one monosyllabic Mandarin word. In terms of the ten disyllabic words, five were tone 3 sandhi words: [tʂu2 jen3] /tʂu3 jen3/ 主演,"to star" (7 repetitions); [tʂu2 ta3] /tʂu3 ta3/ 主打 "hit (describing popular songs)" (1 repetition); [tʂu2 pi3] /tʂu3 pi3/ 主笔 "editorial writer" (1 repetition); [tʂu2 ʂən3] /tʂu3 ʂən3/ 主审 "chief umpire" (1 repetition); [tʂu2 kwan3] /tʂu3 kwan3/ 主管 "chief manager" (1 repetition). Four were tone 3 plus tone 4 words: [tʂu3 zˌən4] /tʂu3 zˌən4/ 主任 "director" (1 repetition); [tʂu3 pan4] /tʂu3 pan4/ 主办 "host" (1 repetition); [tʂu3 li4] /tʂu3 li4/ 主力 "main force" (1 repetition); [tʂu3 je4] /tʂu3 je4/ 主页 "cover page" (7 repetitions). The remaining stimulus consisted of a tone 2 plus a tone 4 syllable: [tʂu2 je4] /tʂu2 je4/ 竹叶 "bamboo leaf" (7 repetitions). The monosyllabic word was [tʂu2] /tʂu2/ 竹 "bamboo" (1 repetition). Notice that the first syllable of the ten disyllabic words and the monosyllabic word were matched on segments.

4.2.3 Design

Four conditions using the oddball paradigm were constructed (See Figure 14). In each condition, 87.5 percent of the stimuli were standards, while 12.5 percent of the stimuli were deviants. In the Tone 2 Condition, 7 physically distinct instances of [tʂu2 je4] /tʂu2 je4/ 竹叶 "bamboo leaf" were used as standards. In the Tone 3 Condition, 7 physically different tokens of [tʂu3 je4] /tʂu3 je4/ 主页 "cover page" were selected as standards. In the Sandhi Condition, 7 physically different instances of [tʂu2 jen3] /tʂu3 jen3/ 主演 "to star" were set as standards. In the Mix Condition, four tone 3 sandhi words ([tʂu2 ta3] /tʂu3 ta3/ 主打 "hit (describing popular songs)"; [tʂu2 pi3] /tʂu3 pi3/ 主笔 "editorial writer"; [tʂu2 ʂən3] /tʂu3 ʂən3/ 主审 "chief umpire"; [tʂu2 kwan3] /tʂu3 kwan3/ 主管 "chief manager") and three disyllabic words with a T3 + T4 tonal sequence ([tʂu3 zˌən4] /tʂu3 zˌən4/ 主任 "director"; [tʂu3 pan4] /tʂu3 pan4/ 主办 "host"; [tʂu3 li4] /tʂu3 li4/ 主力 "main force") were used as standards. For all four conditions, monosyllable [tʂu2] /tʂu2/ 竹 "bamboo" was used as the deviant.

Tone 2 Condition
[tʂu2 jie4]　　　[tʂu2 jie4]······　　[tʂu2]
/tʂu2 jie4/　　　/tʂu2 jie4/　　　　/tʂu2/
"bamboo leaf"

Tone 3 Condition
[tʂu3 jie4]　　　[tʂu3 jie4]······　　[tʂu2]
/tʂu3 jie4/　　　/tʂu3 jie4/　　　　/tʂu2/
"cover page"

Sandhi Condition
[tʂu2 jɛn3]　　　[tʂu2 jɛn3]······　　[tʂu2]
/tʂu3 jɛn3/　　　/tʂu3 jɛn3/　　　　/tʂu2/
"to star"

Mix Condition
[tʂu2 ta3]　[tʂu3 zən4]　[tʂu2 pi3]　[tʂu3 pan4]　[tʂu2 ʂən3]　[tʂu3 li4]　[tʂu2 kwan3]　[tʂu2]
/tʂu3 ta3/　/tʂu3 zən4/　/tʂu3 pi3/　/tʂu3 pan4/　/tʂu3 ʂən3/　/tʂu3 li4/　/tʂu3 kwan3/　/tʂu2/
"to feature"　"manager"　"editorial writer"　"to host"　"umpire"　"main force"　"director"

Figure 14　Stimuli in the Tone 2, Tone 3, Sandhi and Mix Conditions

Note that in the Tone 2 Condition, the first syllable of the standard [tʂu2 je4] /tʂu2 je4/ and the deviant [tʂu2] /tʂu2/ were matched in both the surface and underlying representations, as shown in Figure 6. In the Tone 3 Condition, the first syllable of the standard [tʂu3 je4] /tʂu3 je4/ did not match in tone the deviant [tʂu2] /tʂu2/ in either surface or underlying representation. In the Sandhi Condition, the first syllable of the standard [tʂu2 jen3] /tʂu3 jen3/ shared only the surface representation with the deviant [tʂu2] /tʂu2/. In the Mix Condition, there was not a many-to-one ratio with respect to the first syllable of the standards and the deviant on the surface (both tone 2 and tone

3). However, there was a many-to-one ratio between the first syllable of the standards and the deviant underlyingly (all tone 3). The reason why we included the Mix Condition in addition to the Sandhi Condition was to investigate whether Mandarin listeners could extract a many-to-one ratio in the underlying representation. For the Mix Condition, since there was not a many-to-one ratio on the surface, listeners may be more likely to form a many-to-one ratio at the other level of representation, which was the underlying representation.

Stimulus manipulation was conducted using Praat (Boersma & Weenink, 2013). All the disyllabic stimuli were normalized to 630 ms in duration (first syllable 280 ms + second syllable 350 ms), while the monosyllabic deviant [tṣu2] /tṣu2/ 竹 "bamboo" was 280 ms in duration. Intensity of all stimuli was normalized to 65 dB.

Tonal contours from four canonical tone 2 (four of the seven first syllables of the [tṣu2 je4] /tṣu2 je4/ standards) in the Tone 2 Condition were superimposed upon the first syllable of 4 standards ([tṣu2 jen3] /tṣu3 jen3/) in the Sandhi Condition. Likewise, tonal contours from the three sandhi tones (three of the seven first syllables of the [tṣu2 jen3] /tṣu3 jen3/ standards) in the Sandhi Condition were superimposed on the first syllable of the other 3 standards ([tṣu2 je4] /tṣu2 je4/) in the Tone 2 Condition. Therefore, the first syllable of standards in the Tone 2 and Sandhi Conditions had identical tonal contours.

In the Mix Condition, two of the four standards were the same as the first syllable of the two [tṣu2 je4] /tṣu2 je4/ Tone 2 Condition standards; two of the four were the same as the first syllable of the two [tṣu2 jen3] /tṣu3 jen3/ Sandhi Condition standards. By doing so, the first syllable of standards in the Mix Condition had similar tone 2 contours as the first syllable of standards in the Tone 2 and Sandhi Conditions. In the Tone 3 Condition, tonal contours of the standards were not manipulated. For the deviant, its tonal contour was not manipulated either.

Fundamental frequency (F0) was measured for the seven standard [tṣu2] tokens and the deviant [tṣu2] in the Tone 2 and Sandhi conditions. Similar measures were also collected for the seven standard [tṣu3] tokens in the Tone 3 Condition. Results for [tṣu2] showed that the average fundamental frequency of the seven standard [tṣu2] tokens in the Tone 2 and Sandhi conditions was, on average, 8.66 Hz higher than that of the deviant [tṣu2] in these two conditions (see Figure 15). The ΔF0 value (i.e., the change in fundamental frequency (F0) during the time interval from onset of the tone to the lowest pitch

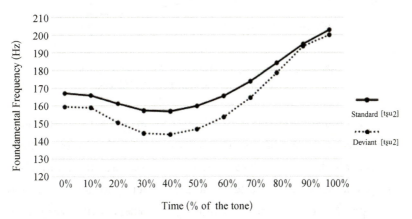

Figure 15 Average Fundamental Frequency Contour of the Seven Standard [tṣu2] Tokens and Fundamental Frequency Contour of the Deviant [tṣu2]

value) of the average F0 contour of the standard [tʂu2] tokens was 10.27 Hz, while the ΔF0 value of the deviant [tʂu2] was 15.51 Hz. For the [tʂu3] tokens, fundamental frequency (F0) was measured for the seven standard [tʂu3] tokens (see Figure 16). The F0 showed that [tʂu3] was realized as a low-falling tone, which was distinct from the tonal contour of the deviant [tʂu2]. Acoustic details of the seven standard [tʂu2] tokens, seven standard [tʂu3] tokens and the deviant [tʂu2] are provided in Appendix 5.

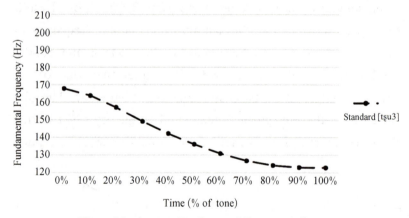

Figure 16　Average Fundamental Frequency Contour of the Seven Standard [tʂu3] Tokens

The four conditions were separately presented in 8 blocks, with each condition being split into two blocks. At the beginning of each block, 14 standards were presented first to familiarize the participants with these standards. Then another 400 trials were presented in a pseudo-randomized order, with every two deviants separated by 2 to 9 standards. There was a 600 ms pause between every two stimuli. In total, participants heard

828 stimuli in each condition, with 728 standards and 100 deviants. A self-paced break was offered between two blocks. The order of the four conditions was counterbalanced across participants.

4.2.4 Procedure

Participants were first invited to the Neurolinguistics & Language Processing Laboratory at The University of Kansas. They filled out a consent form, the Edinburgh Handedness Inventory (Oldfield, 1971), as well as a language background questionnaire. Then the participants was fitted with an electrode cap before they were seated in front of a computer screen. Participants were instructed to ignore auditory stimuli while watching a silent movie with Chinese subtitles. The total duration of the experiment was around 2 hours.

4.2.5 EEG Recordings

EEG was recorded at a sampling rate of 1 kHz using an electrode cap (Electro-cap International, Inc.) from 32 sintered, Ag/AgCl scalp electrodes, arranged in a modified 10-20 layout. Electrode sites were FPz, Fz, FCz, Cz, CPz, Pz, Oz, FP1/2, F7/8, F3/4, FT7/8, FC3/4, T3/4, C3/4, TP7/8, CP3/4, T5/6, P3/4 and O1/2. The recording was amplified by using a Neuroscan Synamps2 amplifier system (Compumedics Neuroscan, Inc.). Polygraphic channels were placed above and below each eye (VEOL and VEOR, individually), and on the left and right outer canthi of each eye (HEO) to detect blinks and eye movements. Impedances were kept below 5 kOhms.

Data were continuously recorded in AC mode using an online high-pass filter of 0.1 Hz and low-pass of 200 Hz.

4.2.6 Data Analysis

ERP analyses were time-locked at the onset of the first syllable of standards (0 ms post onset of standard presentation), the onset of deviants (0 ms post onset of deviant presentation), the onset of the second syllable of standards (280 ms post onset of standard presentation), and the onset of omission positions (280 ms post onset of deviant presentation). Continuous EEG data were first referenced to the left mastoid, and re-referenced offline to linked mastoids. Trials were then epoched by Type (standard and deviant), Condition (Tone 2, Tone 3, Sandhi, and Mix) and Position (first and second syllable of standards, deviant and omission) (-100 ms to 400 ms time window with respect to the time locker (0 ms) for the first-syllable-of-standard epochs and deviant epochs; -400 ms to 400 ms time window with respect to the time locker (0 ms) for the second-syllable-of-standard epochs and omission epochs). The first-syllable-of-standard epochs and deviant epochs were then baseline-corrected regarding the -100 ms to 0 ms interval, while the second-syllable-of-standard epochs and omission epochs were baseline-corrected based on the -380 ms to -280 ms interval. Epochs with amplitudes exceeding ± 100 μV at any channel were automatically rejected; the remaining data were carried forward for further analysis. Averaged ERP waveforms were generated for the first-syllable-of-standard epochs, deviant epochs, second-syllable-of-standard epochs, and omission epochs within each condition.

In terms of onset position analyses, within-condition comparisons were conducted on the mean ERP amplitude elicited by the tone 2 deviant and that yielded by the first syllable of standards within each condition. Any comparison in the 100 ms and 300 ms time window showing that the deviant was more negative than the first syllable of standards (we considered $p < .05$ to be significant, and $.05 < p < .1$ to be marginal) would be evidence for effects of mismatch negativity. With regard to between-condition comparisons, mean ERP amplitude elicited by the tone 2 deviant in the Tone 2 Condition was selected as a baseline to which mean ERP amplitude yielded by the tone 2 deviant in the other three conditions were compared.

For omission position analyses, within-condition comparisons were conducted on mean ERP amplitude elicited by the omission position and that yielded by the second syllable of standards within each condition. Any comparison in the 100 ms and 300 ms time window showing that the omission was more negative than the second syllable of standards (we considered $p < .05$ to be significant, and $.05 < p < .1$ to be marginal) would be evidence for effects of mismatch negativity. With respect to the between-condition comparisons, mean ERP amplitude elicited by the omission position in the Tone 2 condition were chosen as a baseline to which mean ERP amplitude yielded by the omission position in the other three conditions were compared. In total, there were 8 within-condition comparisons and 6 between-condition comparisons.

The midline electrode Fz was selected for mean ERP

amplitude analyses since previous studies have shown that mismatch effects have a fronto-central distribution (Näätänen et al., 2007; Gu et al., 2012; Ren et al., 2009). For each participant, mean ERP amplitude was calculated by averaging the ERP voltages in the 100 ms and 300 ms time window across epochs by Type (standard vs. deviant), Condition (Tone 2, Tone 3, Sandhi, and Mix) and Position (first syllable vs. second syllable/omission).

4.3 Predictions

4.3.1 Onset

For the within-condition comparisons between deviants (tone 2) and the first syllable of standards, we would not expect to observe any MMN effect in the Tone 2 Condition due to the match between the two in tone in both underlying and surface representations (see Figure 14).

For the Tone 3 Condition, we would expect to observe an MMN effect due to the mismatch between the two in both underlying and surface representations (see Figure 14) although Li and Chen (2015) found a reduced MMN effect when a tone 3 monosyllable was the standard and a tone 2 monosyllable was the deviant. In the current study, disyllabic standards starting with a tone 3 might reduce the possibility for Mandarin-speaking participants to activate a tone 2 when hearing an initial tone 3 because the initial tone 3 syllable was not followed by another tone 3 syllable, which would allow the participants to assign a clear and firm tone 3 interpretation for it, potentially leading to a stronger MMN effect.

For the Sandhi Condition, an MMN effect would be predicted depending on how participants represent and process Mandarin tone 3 sandhi words. If they process Mandarin tone 3 sandhi words mainly based on the underlying representation, an MMN effect would be elicited since there is a many-to-one ratio between the tone of deviants and that of the first syllable of standards, underlyingly. If they only focus on the surface representation of Mandarin tone 3 sandhi words, then no MMN effect would be expected due to the lack of tonal mismatch with the tone 2 deviant (see Figure 14).

In terms of the Mix Condition, an MMN effect would be observed depending on whether Mandarin-speaking participants could extract the underlying tone of the first syllable of standards despite the differences in the surface tone. If they can, then an MMN effect would be produced because there is a many-to-one ratio between the tone of the deviants and that of the first syllable of the standards in the underlying representation. If they cannot, then no MMN effect would be elicited (see Figure 14).

Regarding the between-condition comparisons for deviants across conditions, we predicted the most negative ERPs for the deviant in the Tone 3 Condition given the surface and underlying tone mismatch in the within-condition comparison between the first syllable of standards and the deviant. Moreover, we predicted that ERPs elicited by the deviants in the Tone 2 and Mix Conditions would be less negative than those yielded by the deviant in the Tone 3 Condition given that the within-condition comparisons in the Tone 2 and Mix Condition might fail to yield MMN effects. Finally, we predicted that the degree of negativity elicited by the deviant in the Sandhi Condition should depend on the presence or absence of MMN effects in the within-condition comparison in this condition. If we observed an MMN effect in the Sandhi Condition for the within-condition comparison, then we would expect more negative ERPs yielded by the deviants in the Sandhi Condition than those in the Tone 2 Condition. If we did not obtain any MMN effect in the Sandhi Condition for the within-condition comparison, then we would predict similar degrees of negativity generated by the deviants in the Sandhi and Tone 2 conditions.

4.3.2 Omission

For the within-condition comparisons between the omission position and the second syllable of standards, we predicted to observe omission MMN effects in the Tone 2, Tone 3, Sandhi, and Mix Conditions given that the deviant is a monosyllable, which would violate the regularity or prediction formed by the disyllabic standards (Raij et al., 1997; Yabe et al., 1997; Yabe et al., 1998; Janata, 2001).

In terms of the between-condition comparisons for the omission position across conditions, we expected that the ERPs yielded by the omission position in the Tone 2, Tone 3 and Sandhi Conditions would show similar degrees of negativity since the second syllable of standards in these three conditions does not vary in each condition, allowing participants to actively predict what they would hear as the next stimulus. In addition, ERPs elicited by the omission position in the Mix Condition would show a weaker negativity than those yielded by the omission position in the Tone 2 Condition due to participants' inability to predict the segmental content of the second syllable of standards in the Mix Condition (Bendixen et al., 2014; Bendixen, SanMiguel, & Schröger, 2012).

4.4 Results

4.4.1 Mean ERP Amplitude for the Onset and the First Syllable of Standards

Statistical analyses were conducted on the mean ERP amplitude obtained from the MMN experiment. Eight participants' data were discarded due to excessive artifacts (i.e., over 50 deviant trials out of 100, both onset and omission positions, excluded by automatic artifact rejection). The remaining 12 participants' data were subjected to statistical analyses.

A series of linear mixed-effects analyses were conducted on the participants' mean ERP amplitude generated by the deviants and the first syllable of standards within a 100 – 300 ms time window using the lme4 package in R (Bates et al., 2015).

For the within-condition comparisons between deviants and the first syllable of standards, participants' Mean ERP Amplitude was regarded as a dependent variable, while Type (First Syllable of Standard and Deviant) was set categorically as an independent variable. For Type, Deviant was selected as the baseline to which First Syllable of Standard was compared in order to examine MMN effects. Participant was treated as a random effect. One such model was created for each condition. All significant effects ($p < .05$) and trends ($p < .10$) are reported.

Results of within-condition comparisons between the first syllable of standards and the deviants in the 100-300 ms time window showed that ERPs elicited by the deviants in the Tone 2 condition were more negative than those yielded by the First Syllable of Standards in the same condition ($\beta = 0.943$, SE = .510, $t = 1.848$, $p = .091$) (see Figure 17a), showing an MMN effect. ERPs yielded by the deviants in the Tone 3 condition were also significantly more negative than those produced by the First Syllable of Standards in the same condition ($\beta = 1.794$, SE = .397, $t = 4.515$, $p < .001$) (see Figure 17b), again, confirming an MMN effect. However, ERPs elicited by the deviants in the Sandhi condition were not significantly different from those yielded by the First Syllable of Standards in the same condition ($\beta = -.064$, SE = .343, $t =$

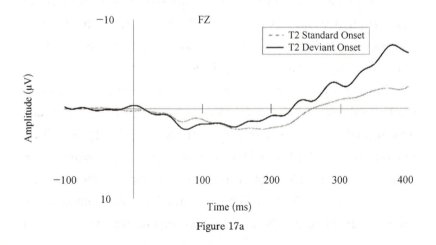

Figure 17a

Chapter 4 An ERP Study on Mandarin Tone 3 Sandhi Processing

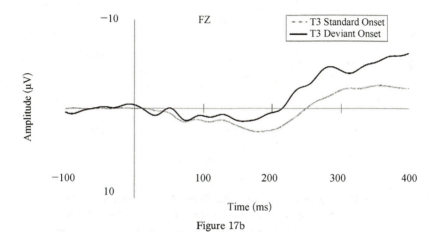

Figure 17b

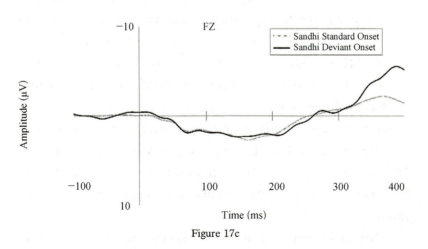

Figure 17c

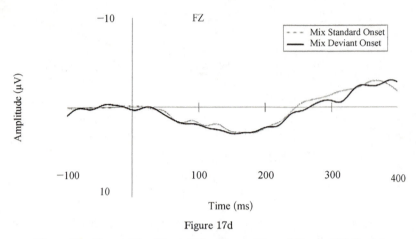

Figure 17d

Figure 17 Figure 17a, Figure 17b, Figure 17c and Figure 17d Depict Mean ERP Waveforms Averaged across 12 Participants in the 0-400 ms Time Window Using the −100-0 ms Time Window as the Baseline. Electrode FZ Was Selected

−.187, $p = .855$) (see Figure 17c), nor were ERPs yielded by the deviants in the Mix condition compared with those produced by the First Syllable of Standards in the same condition ($\beta = -.310$, SE $= .350$, $t = -.886$, $p = .394$) (see Figure 17d).

For the between-condition comparisons of deviants, participants' Mean ERP Amplitude was set as a dependent variable. Condition was treated as a categorical independent variable (Tone 2, Tone 3, Sandhi, and Mix). For Condition, Tone 2 was chosen as the baseline to which Tone 3, Sandhi, and Mix were compared. Participant was treated as a random variable.

Results of between-condition comparisons of deviants in the 100-300 ms time window showed a main effect of Condition ($F(3, 33) = 7.05$, $p < .001$), indicating that Condition is a factor in influencing the mean ERP amplitude of deviants. Pairwise comparisons demonstrated that ERPs elicited by the deviants in the Tone 3 condition were more negative than those yielded in the Tone 2 condition ($\beta = -1.100$, SE = .577, $t = -1.908$, $p = .065$) (see Figure 18a). Also, ERPs elicited by the deviants in the Tone 2 condition were more negative than those yielded in both the Sandhi Condition ($\beta = 1.035$, SE =

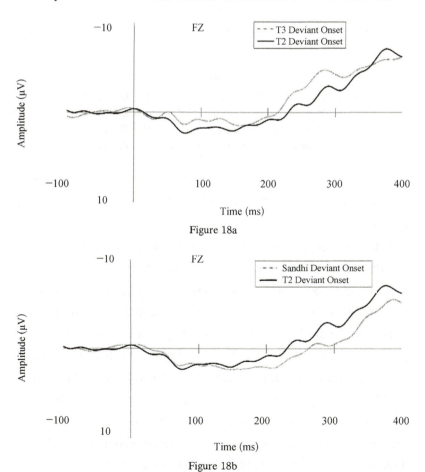

Figure 18a

Figure 18b

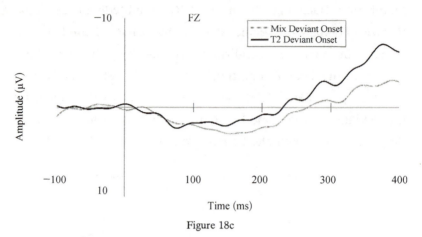

Figure 18c

Figure 18 Figure 18a, Figure 18b and Figure 18c Depict Mean ERP Waveforms Averaged across 12 Participants in the 0-400 ms Time Window Using the −100-0 ms Time Window as the Baseline. Electrode FZ Was Selected

.577, $t = 1.795$, $p = .08$) (See Figure 18b) and the Mix condition ($\beta = 1.262$, SE = .577, $t = 2.189$, $p = .036$) (see Figure 18c).

The results for the within-and between-condition comparisons for the onset position are summarized in Figure 19. For the within-condition comparisons, MMN effects are observed in the 100-300 ms time window for the Tone 2 and Tone 3 conditions, indicating that Mandarin speaking participants treated the deviants in the Tone 2 and Tone 3 Conditions differently from the first syllable of standards in these two conditions. However, no MMN effect was observed in the 100-300 ms time window for the Sandhi and Mix Conditions. For the Sandhi and Mix Conditions, Mandarin speaking participants seem to process the deviant and the first syllable of standards similarly.

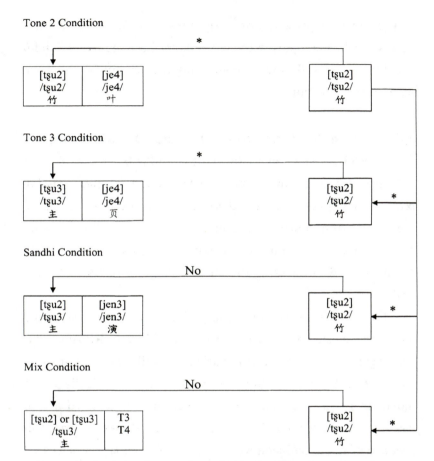

Figure 19 Statistical Results of the Within-Condition Comparisons between the First Syllable of Standards and the Deviant in Each Condition as Well as the Statistical Results of the Between-Condition Comparisons for Deviants across Conditions. Asterisks Indicate Significant Effects and Trends

For the between-condition comparisons, the data show that the deviant in the Tone 3 Condition produced the most negative mean ERP amplitude, with the deviant in the Tone 3 Condition mismatching the first syllable of standards in both underlying and surface representation. Significant effects were also observed when comparing the deviants in the Tone 2 and Sandhi Conditions, as well as when comparing the deviants in the Tone 2 and Mix Conditions.

4.4.2 Mean ERP Amplitude for the Omission Position and the Second Syllable of Standards

In order to examine the effects elicited by the omission position, a series of linear-mixed effects analyses were conducted on the participants' mean ERP amplitude elicited by the omission position and the second syllable of standards within a 100 – 300 ms time window using the lme4 package in R (Bates et al., 2015).

For the within-condition comparisons between deviants and the second syllable of standards, participants' Mean ERP Amplitude was regarded as a dependent variable, while Type (Omission and Second Syllable of Standard) was set categorically as an independent variable. For Type, Omission was selected as the baseline to which Second Syllable of Standard was compared in order to evaluate omission MMN effects. Participant was treated as a random effect. Four such models were generated.

Results of within-condition comparisons between the mean ERP amplitude yielded by the omission position and that elicited by the second syllable of standards in the 100 – 300 ms time window reached significance in the Tone 2 Condition (β = 2.480, SE = .669, t = 3.709, p = .003) (see Figure 20a), Tone 3 Condition (β = 3.030, SE = .847, t = 3.578, p = .004) (see Figure 20b), Sandhi condition (β =

1.727, SE = .821, t = 2.105, p = .059) (see Figure 20c), and Mix condition (β = 1.448, SE = .507, t = 2.854, p = .016) (Figure 20d). The results showed that the omission position produced more negative mean ERP amplitude than the second syllable of standards for all comparisons (omission MMN effects).

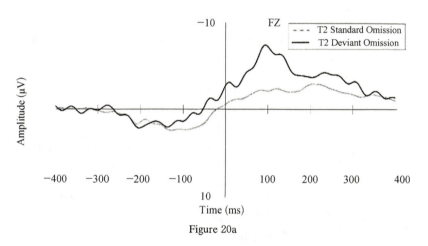

Figure 20a

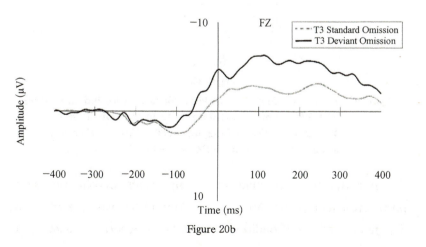

Figure 20b

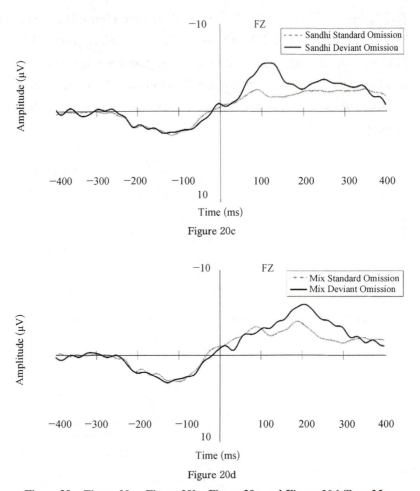

Figure 20 Figure 20a, Figure 20b, Figure 20c and Figure 20d Show Mean ERP Waveforms Averaged across 12 Participants in the 0–400 ms Time Window Using the −380– −280 ms Time Window as the Baseline. Electrode FZ Was Selected

For the between-condition comparisons of the omission position, participants' Mean ERP Amplitude was treated as a dependent variable. Condition was set as a categorical independent variable (Tone 2, Tone 3, Sandhi, and Mix). For Condition, Tone 2 was chosen as the baseline to which Tone 3, Sandhi, and Mix were compared. Participant was regarded a random variable.

Results of between-condition comparisons of omissions in the 100-300 ms time window showed a significant main effect of Condition ($F(3, 33) = 2.344$, $p = .091$), indicating that Condition was a factor in influencing Mean ERP Amplitude. Subsequent pairwise comparisons, however, did not demonstrate any significant effects between the omission in the Tone 2 Condition and the omission in either of the other three conditions (omission T2 vs. T3 conditions: $\beta = -.771$, SE = .708, $t = -1.090$, $p = .284$ (see Figure 21a); omission T2 vs. Sandhi conditions: $\beta = .956$, SE = .708, $t = 1.351$, $p = .186$ (see Figure 21b); omission T2 vs. Mix conditions: $\beta = .654$, SE = .708, $t = .925$, $p = .362$ (see Figure 21c)).

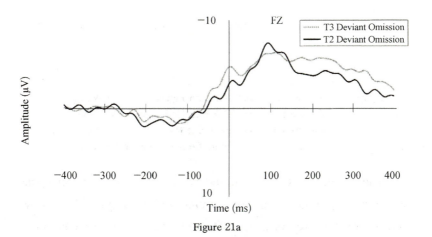

Figure 21a

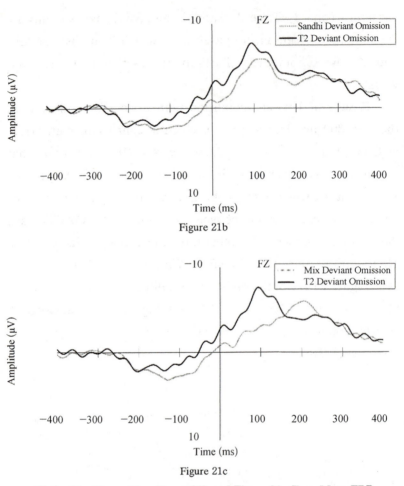

Figure 21   Figure 21a, Figure 21b and Figure 21c Show Mean ERP Waveforms Averaged across 12 Participants in the 0–400 ms Time Window Using the −380– −280 ms Time Window as the Baseline. Electrode FZ Was Selected

The results for the within-and between-condition comparisons at the omission position are summarized in Figure 22 below. Overall, we observed omission MMN effects for all four conditions

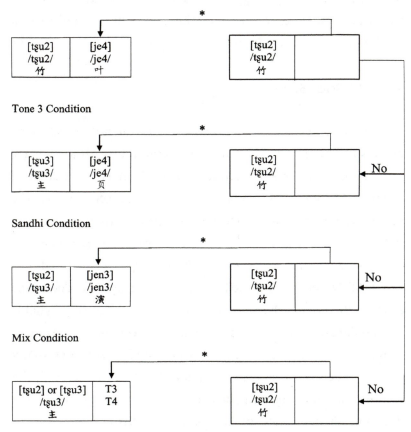

Figure 22 Statistical Results of the Within-Condition Comparisons between the Second Syllable of Standards and the Omission in Each Condition as Well as the Statistical Results of the Between-Condition Comparisons for Omissions across Conditions. Asterisks Indicate Significant Effects and Trends

when comparing the mean ERP amplitude elicited by the omission position with that yielded by the second syllable of standards within the same condition (100 – 300 ms time window). For between-condition comparisons, no significant difference was observed when comparing the omission position in the Tone 2 Condition with that in either of the other three conditions in the 100-300 ms time window.

4.5 Discussion

The current study investigated how Mandarin speakers process and represent Mandarin tone 3 sandhi words at an early stage of language comprehension. In particular, we examined whether Mandarin speakers would be more sensitive to the surface representation or underlying representation of the first syllable of tone 3 sandhi words ([tone 2 tone 3]/tone 3 tone 3/).

Our results showed an MMN effect in the Tone 2 Condition. The MMN effect in the tone 2 condition is most likely due to the acoustic differences between the deviants and the first syllable of standards. This significant MMN effect in the Tone 2 Condition is consistent with previous studies showing MMN effects when deviants and standards differed acoustically (within the same phoneme category) but not phonemically (in different phoneme categories) (Xi et al., 2010).

We also found a significant difference between the Tone 2 and Sandhi Conditions in that within-condition comparisons (comparing the deviant with the first syllable of standards) demonstrated an MMN effect in the Tone 2 Condition, but not in the Sandhi Condition. Notice that the acoustic information of the first syllable of standards in these two conditions was identical. Moreover, the deviants used in these two conditions were also identical. Nevertheless, we only observed an MMN effect in the Tone 2 Condition but not in the Sandhi Condition. We suggest disparate neural mechanisms when processing tone 2 standards ([tṣu2 je4] /tṣu2 je4/) and sandhi standards ([tṣu2 jen3] /tṣu3 jen3/).

The lack of such an effect in the Sandhi Condition may be due to the representation of Mandarin tone 3 sandhi. Recall that Mandarin tone 3 sandhi is triggered by a phonological environment, that is, a tone 3 syllable undergoes tone sandhi, changing into a tone 2 syllable when followed by another tone 3 syllable. For our sandhi condition, participants heard many tone 3 sandhi words ([tṣu2 jen3] /tṣu3 jen3/). Since no MMN effect was observed when hearing a tone 2 deviant in the Sandhi Condition, participants seem to be assigning an underspecified representation for the first syllable of those tone 3 sandhi words. It is not until they encounter the tone of the second syllable of the standards do they have to decide whether they should interpret the tone of the first syllable as an underlying tone 2 (/tṣu2/) or an underlying tone 3 (/tṣu3/) syllable, that is, an underspecified representation. Given this assignment of an underspecified representation, the deviant ([tṣu2] /tṣu2/) does not elicit an MMN effect even though the acoustic differences between the first syllable of sandhi standards and the deviant could have yielded it, as observed in the tone 2 condition.

Another possibility for the lack of MMN effects in the Sandhi Condition may be because participants systematically applied the tone 3 sandhi rule consistently, changing the initial surface tone 2 into an underlying tone 3, with no exceptions (even for the deviant [tṣu2]). Given that participants heard many sandhi words in this condition, they may predict the upcoming stimulus to be a sandhi word, thus changing the surface [tṣu2] into the underlying /tṣu3/. By doing so, they process the first syllable in a trial as an underlying tone 3. Therefore, when hearing the deviant [tṣu2], participants treat it as /tṣu3/, which is not in conflict with the first syllable of standards ([tṣu2 jen3] /tṣu3 jen3/), resulting in no MMN effect.

Regarding the MMN effect in the Tone 3 Condition (comparing the deviant with the first syllable of tone 3 standards), we observed a strong MMN effect. This MMN effect resulted from the mismatch between the tone of the first syllable of standards ([tṣu3 je4] /tṣu3 je4/) in the Tone 3 Condition and the tone of deviants ([tṣu2] /tṣu2/) in both underlying and surface representations. Being regularly exposed to the standard [tṣu3 je4] /tṣu3 je4/ in the Tone 3 Condition, Mandarin-speaking participants interpret the first syllable they hear in a trial to be tone 3. When encountering the deviant [tṣu2] /tṣu2/, this acoustic signal violated the stored regularity (or the prediction), eliciting a significantly more negative ERP waveform relative to that yielded by the first syllable of tone 3 standards ([tṣu3 je4] /tṣu3 je4/) in the Tone 3 Condition.

For the Mix Condition, we did not observe an MMN effect when comparing the first syllable of standards with the deviant. Our design in this condition demonstrated a many-to-one ratio only in the underlying representation between the first syllable of standards (/tṣu3/) and the deviant (/tṣu2/). If Mandarin-speaking participants pay attention to the underlying representation and abstract away from the surface variability, an MMN effect would have been observed. The lack of an MMN effect in the Mix Condition indicated that participants were not sensitive to the many-to-one ratio in the underlying representation, or at least they could not extract the underlying many-to-one ratio to generate a significant MMN effect, focusing instead on the surface tonal variability. The combination of tone 2 and tone 3 for the first syllable of standards on the surface in the Mix Condition may make it difficult for the participants to form a regularity concerning the tone of the first syllable.

The current study used disyllabic Mandarin tone 3 sandhi words to investigate how Mandarin speakers process the first syllable of tone 3 sandhi words, which is a tone 2 on the surface. In Mandarin, around 70 percent of words are disyllabic (Shei, 2014), and Mandarin tone 3 sandhi is conditioned in a certain phonological context. By using disyllabic tone 3 sandhi words as stimuli, we can better simulate how Mandarin speakers process tone 3 sandhi words in daily conversation.

The current data differ from the study of Li and Chen (2015) in that Li and Chen (2015) focused on how Mandarin speakers process tone 3 monosyllables and only made inferences regarding the tonal alternation phenomenon between Mandarin tone 2 and tone 3. Using these data on monosyllabic processing, Li and Chen (2015) proposed that Mandarin tone 3 may be represented as both tone 2 and tone 3 in the mental lexicon. Li and Chen (2015) found a reduced MMN effect when tone 3 monosyllables were the standard and tone 2 monosyllables were the deviant compared to when tone 2 monosyllables were the standard and tone 3 monosyllables were the deviant. The reduced MMN effect in Li and Chen (2015) was attributed to the parallel activation of both tone 2 and tone 3 when hearing tone 3 monosyllables as the standard. For Li and Chen, when Mandarin speakers encountered the tone 2 deviant, it did not substantially violate the memory traces formed by the standard, resulting in a reduced MMN effect.

The current data using disyllables, however, present a different picture. Using disyllables, we observed a very strong MMN effect in the Tone 3 Condition in which the disyllabic word [tşu3 je4] /tşu3 je4/ was the standard and the monosyllable [tşu2] /tşu2/ was the deviant. We also found a significantly more negative mean ERP amplitude elicited by the deviant in the Tone 3 Condition compared to that in the Tone 2 Condition. In the Tone 3 Condition of the present study, the initial tone of the standard [tşu3 je4] /tşu3 je4/ is clearly specified since it was always followed by a tone 4 syllable. The initial tone 3 of the standard was not in the phonological environment to trigger tone 3 sandhi. Thus, a tone 2 representation for the first syllable of [tşu3 je4] /tşu3 je4/ could not be activated, with only a tone 3 representation viable. Therefore, a strong MMN effect was observed when the deviant [tşu2] /tşu2/ violated the regularity, mismatching the first syllable of [tşu3 je4] /tşu3 je4/ in both surface and underlying representation.

For the omission position, we observed MMN effects across all conditions. The omission MMN effect has also been reported in the previous literature (Raij et al., 1997; Yabe et al., 1997; Yabe et al., 1998; Janata, 2001; Bendixen, Schröger, & Winkler,

2009; Bendixen et al., 2014). Our current data show omission MMN effects in all four conditions, suggesting that participants processed all the stimuli as disyllabic words, including the monosyllabic deviants. Therefore, when they did not hear the second syllable, an MMN effect was generated. Thus, our within-condition comparison results (comparing the omission position with the second syllable of standards) demonstrated robust omission MMN effects, which can be explained by either violation of previous regularity formed in the memory (Näätänen et al., 1997; Näätänen et al., 2007) or violation of prediction of existence of the second syllable (Bendixen et al., 2014; Bendixen, SanMiguel, & Schröger, 2012).

For the between-condition comparisons at the omission position, we did not obtain any effect when comparing the mean ERP amplitude elicited by the deviant in the Tone 2 Condition with that in the Tone 3, Sandhi and Mix Conditions in the 100-300 ms time window. These results suggest that participants employ similar neural processing mechanisms handling the omission position in these conditions. Participants either formed a regular pattern that all the stimuli were disyllabic and anticipated a second syllable, or actively predicted possible segmental and tonal contents for the second syllable.

Taken together, the current results suggest different neural mechanisms for processing canonical tone 2 syllables and sandhi tone 2 syllables in the initial position of disyllabic words. When processing tone 3 sandhi words, Mandarin speakers either assign an underspecified representation to the tone 2 syllable of Mandarin tone 3 sandhi words, or employ the tone 3 sandhi rule to change the initial tone 2 syllable into a tone 3 syllable for lexical access.

4.6 Conclusion

The present study investigated how Mandarin tone sandhi words are processed at a very early stage of language comprehension. Our results support the existence of predictive coding mechanisms in the central auditory system to aid spoken word recognition. Our data also showed different neural processing mechanisms involved in the processing of canonical tone 2 syllables and sandhi tone 2 syllables in disyllabic sequences. We proposed two possibilities for the processing of Mandarin tone 3 sandhi words: An underspecified tonal representation assigned to the first syllable of Mandarin tone 3 sandhi words, or an underlying representation /tone 3 tone 3/ in which initial surface tone 2 syllable is converted into an underlying tone 3 syllable using the tone 3 sandhi rule (computational mechanism).

Chapter 5
General Discussion and Conclusion

5.0 Summary

This book investigated how native Mandarin and Southern Min speakers process tone sandhi words. Tone sandhi is a phonological alternation phenomenon in which a tone changes to a different tone in certain phonological environments, such that the surface acoustic information mismatches the underlying linguistic representation. Therefore, tone sandhi is an excellent test case to examine the role of the surface and underlying representations during lexical access, namely, whether speakers store the surface form of tone sandhi words in the mental lexicon and access it during spoken word recognition, or whether they store the abstract linguistic representation of tone sandhi words and employ a computational mechanism to convert the surface form into the underlying representation for lexical access. Given that the nature of tone sandhi systems has been shown to influence tone sandhi productivity (Zhang & Lai, 2010; Zhang, Lai, & Sailor; 2011), we are also interested in whether tone sandhi words with disparate sandhi characteristics would be processed and represented differently. We used two psycholinguistic auditory priming experiments and a neurolinguistic mismatch negativity experiment to tap into different stages of tone sandhi word processing. Additionally, we chose Mandarin tone 3 sandhi (transparent, phonotactically motivated), Southern Min tone sandhi 24 → 33 (opaque, phonotactically motivated), and Southern Min tone sandhi 51 → 55 (opaque, lacking phonotactic motivation) to investigate whether sandhi words with different tone sandhi characteristics would be processed and represented differently. Our data shed light on the nature of the representation of tone sandhi words within the same language, and across different languages, as well as informing models of spoken word recognition.

The first experiment in the book investigated the processing of Mandarin tone 3 sandhi words, using an auditory-auditory priming lexical decision task. The second experiment examined the processing of two different Southern Min tone sandhis (T51 → T55 and T24 → T33), using a similar experimental methodology and design. The final study investigated early brain responses to Mandarin tone 3 sandhi words using mismatch negativity.

5.1 Tone Sandhi Word Processing and Representation in the Mental Lexicon

Experiment 1 focused on the transparent and phonotactically motivated Mandarin tone 3 sandhi and examined how words undergoing Mandarin tone 3 sandhi are processed and represented in the mental lexicon. In this study, we found that participants' lexical decision times to Mandarin tone 3 sandhi targets were significantly facilitated when the primes and the first syllable of targets matched in tone underlyingly. Moreover, surface tonal overlap between the primes and the first syllable of targets did not facilitate participants' lexical decision responses. In addition, we observed that both high frequency and low frequency Mandarin tone 3 sandhi targets elicited identical reaction time patterns, with the tone 3 condition (underlying tone overlap condition) yielding significant facilitative effects relative to the unrelated control, while the tone 2 condition (surface tone overlap condition) was not distinct from the unrelated control condition. The data suggest that Mandarin tone 3 sandhi words are processed based on their underlying representation during spoken word recognition, and are represented as /tone 3 tone 3/ in the mental lexicon.

Our Mandarin priming data is consistent with previous productivity studies on Mandarin tone 3 sandhi (Zhang & Lai, 2010; Zhang, Xia, & Peng, 2015) in that Mandarin tone 3 sandhi productions engage the underlying representation, namely, the underlying tone 3 for the first syllable of the sandhi words. In these two production studies, Mandarin speakers were presented with two tone 3 monosyllables and asked to produce them as a disyllabic chunk, so that productivity of the Mandarin tone 3 sandhi rule could be investigated. Their results showed that the Mandarin tone 3 sandhi rule applied without exception to both real words and pseudo-words, indicating a computational mechanism for the production processing of Mandarin tone 3 sandhi words rather than a process of allomorph selection between a tone 3 morpheme and its tone 2 variant (accidental gap syllables don't have listed allomorphs). The current

Mandarin priming data complement the previous production studies on Mandarin tone 3 sandhi word processing, demonstrating that the transparent, phonotactically motivated and extremely productive Mandarin tone 3 sandhi is processed and represented with respect to its underlying representation in perception. During spoken word recognition, the surface representation of Mandarin tone 3 sandhi words [tone 2 tone 3] needs to be converted into the underlying representation /tone 3 tone 3/, and the underlying form is then used for lexical access. Our Mandarin data further show that word frequency is not a factor in influencing how Mandarin tone 3 sandhi words are processed: both high and low frequency tone 3 sandhi words are processed and represented as /tone 3 tone 3/.

Experiment 2 investigated how Southern Min words with two distinct tone sandhis (51 → 55 and 24 → 33) are processed and represented in the mental lexicon. Taiwanese tone sandhi is very different from Mandarin tone 3 sandhi in that Southern Min tone sandhi is opaque, operating in a circular-chain-shift fashion (see Figure 9). Moreover, even within Southern Min tone sandhi itself, there is a difference between sandhi 51 → 55 and sandhi 24 → 33, with the latter having a phonotactic motivation but not the former since Southern Min phonotactics does not allow tone 24 to occur in the non-phrase final position, but it is phonotactically legal for tone 51 to appear in the non-phrase final position (sandhi 21 → 51). Therefore, phonotactically speaking, it is not necessary for tone 51 to be changed in the non-phrase final position in Southern Min. Previous productivity studies have shown that Southern Min tone sandhi is not as productive as Mandarin tone 3 sandhi in a nonword generation test (Zhang, Lai, & Sailor, 2011), yielding only 80% correct application for Southern Min tone sandhi 24 → 33, and only 40% correct application for Southern Min tone sandhi 51 → 55. Given these differences between Mandarin tone 3 sandhi and Southern Min tone sandhi, as well as between Southern Min tone sandhi 51 → 55 and 24 → 33, we expected to observe different contributions from the surface and underlying representation for Southern Min tone sandhi.

We indeed observed very different patterns between Mandarin tone 3 sandhi and Southern Min tone sandhi. We also obtained significant differences in reaction times between Southern Min tone sandhi 24 → 33 and tone sandhi 51 → 55. For Southern Min tone sandhi 24 → 33, we found that both underlying and surface tone overlap between primes and the first syllable of tone sandhi targets significantly facilitated participants' lexical decision responses, with the underlying facilitative priming effect being significantly larger than the surface facilitation effect. For Southern Min tone sandhi 51 → 55, in contrast, although we observed that both underlying and surface tone overlap between primes and the first syllable of tone sandhi targets facilitated participants' lexical decision responses, the surface facilitative priming effect was significantly larger than the underlying facilitation effect.

Considering the Mandarin and Southern Min data in the previous literature and the current studies together, a relationship between the productivity of tone sandhi and the contributions of the surface and underlying representations can be observed. For extremely productive tone sandhi like Mandarin tone 3 sandhi, since speakers of the language exceptionlessly apply the sandhi rule (100%), they encode and decode tone sandhi words with reference to the underlying representation. A computational mechanism is involved for speakers to generate correct surface forms of extremely productive sandhi process without exception (Zhang, Xia, & Peng, 2015).

For a slightly less productive tone sandhi like Southern Min tone sandhi 24 → 33, speakers can use the tone sandhi rule, but this computational mechanism generating correct sandhi surface forms is not automatic. Our priming data show that they also need to process the surface representation of sandhi words as well, and may even store the surface representation in the mental lexicon. Upon hearing these tone sandhi 24 → 33 words, both underlying and surface representations must be activated, with the underlying representation still contributing to a greater extent via the computational mechanism.

For the least productive sandhi like Southern Min tone sandhi 51 → 55, speakers seem to rely on the surface representation, which contributes to processing to a greater extent. However, the underlying representation also contributes, but to a lesser extent. They have to store the surface form of these least productive sandhi words in the mental lexicon.

The Mandarin and Southern Min priming data show varying contributions of surface and underlying representations, as they are accessed in a gradient fashion rather than in an all-or-nothing way for the processing of tone sandhi words. The surface and underlying contributions are modulated by characteristics of tone sandhi, such as opacity/transparency and phonotactic motivation, across different languages and even within the same language. The current priming data for Mandarin tone 3 sandhi and Southern Min tone sandhi shed light on how speakers process sandhi words with distinctive tone sandhi properties and on how the mental lexicon organizes these tone sandhi words. We propose that the transparent, phonotactically motivated and extremely productive Mandarin tone 3 sandhi is processed and represented as /tone 3 tone 3/. The opaque, phonotactically motivated, and slightly less productive Southern Min words are processed and represented as both /tone 24 tone X/ and /tone 33 tone X/, with the underlying representation /tone 24 tone X/ playing a more important role. The opaque, phonotactically unmotivated and least productive Southern Min tone sandhi 51 → 55 is processed and represented as /tone 51 tone X/ and /tone 55 tone X/, with the surface representation /tone 55 tone X/ being substantially more important during spoken word recognition.

In addition to the productive nature of tone sandhi that impacts the processing and representation of tone sandhi words, a secondary factor, word frequency, also contributes. While our data show an influence of frequency on the opaque and phonotactically motivated tone sandhi (Southern Min sandhi 24 → 33) and for the opaque and phonotactically unmotivated tone sandhi (Southern Min sandhi 51 → 55), we do not observe an interaction of Prime X Frequency for the transparent and phonotactically motivated tone sandhi (Mandarin tone 3 sandhi). The lack of the Prime X Frequency interaction effect on the processing of Mandarin tone 3 sandhi words results from the productive computational mechanism limiting the influence of word frequency on the underlying representation.

For Southern Min tone sandhi, the results suggest that within the global effect showing mainly underlying tone priming for tone sandhi 24 → 33 and mainly surface tone priming for tone sandhi 51 → 55, word frequency contributes differently across these two sandhi types, with different effects for underlying and surface primes. Comparing these sandhis, it appears that surface priming is modulated more by frequency than the underlying priming. One caveat when directly comparing the frequency effect for tone sandhi 24 → 33 and tone sandhi 51 → 55 is that the tone sandhi words were sparsely sampled across these two sandhi types, resulting in slightly different frequency distributions. Therefore, it is difficult to draw strong conclusions concerning how word frequency impacts the processing of tone sandhi words in Southern Min. However, the most crucial information revealed from the current data is that the underlying tone contributes much more than the surface tone for the opaque and phonotactically motivated tone sandhi, and the surface tone contributes much more than the underlying tone for the opaque and phonotactically unmotivated tone sandhi, with word frequency operating differently depending on the contribution of the surface representation for these two sandhi types.

5.2 Tone Sandhi Word Processing at a Very Early Stage of Language Comprehension

Experiment 3 examined how Mandarin speakers process

Mandarin tone 3 sandhi word at a very early stage of language comprehension using the mismatch negativity methodology. In particular, we focused on how Mandarin speakers handle the initial tone 2 syllable of disyllabic Mandarin tone 3 sandhi words. Tone 2, Tone 3, Sandhi, and Mix Conditions were created in which the tonal information of the first syllable was contrasted. In the Tone 2 Condition, disyllabic standards began with a tone 2 syllable ([tṣu2 je4] /tṣu2 je4/). In the Tone 3 Condition, disyllabic standards started with a tone 3 syllable ([tṣu3 je4] /tṣu3 je4/). In the Sandhi Condition, disyllabic standards began with a surface tone 2 syllable ([tṣu2 jen3] /tṣu3 jen3/). In the Mix Condition, disyllabic standards started with either a tone 2 or a tone 3 syllable ([tṣu2 X3] /tṣu3 X3/ or [tṣu3 X4] /tṣu3 X4/). A tone 2 deviant [tṣu2] occurred for all conditions. A crucial manipulation for this study was to control the tonal information of the first syllable in the tone 2 and sandhi words. If Mandarin speakers only process the surface representation, the speakers should show the same results across Tone 2 and Sandhi Conditions.

We found different neural processing mechanisms for tone 2 words ([tone 2 tone 4] /tone 2 tone 4/) versus tone 3 sandhi words ([tone 2 tone 3] /tone 3 tone 3/) in that mean ERP amplitude elicited by the deviant was more negative than that yielded by the first syllable of standards only in the Tone 2 Condition (MMN), but not in the Sandhi Condition (no MMN). For the Sandhi Condition, although the first syllable had the same tone 2 information as in the Tone 2 Condition, the MMN effect occurred in the sandhi context, not in the [tone 2 tone 4] context. We propose that the lack of MMN effects is due to Mandarin participants' sensitivity to the underlying representation but not to the surface representation. If participants had been processing the surface representation, one would have expected an MMN effect in the sandhi condition, as was found in the Tone 2 Condition. We suggest that since the stimuli in the Sandhi condition were [tşu2 jen3] /tşu3 jen3/, Mandarin participants were predicting the incoming stimulus to be a tone sandhi word. Under such circumstances, they engage a computational mechanism, converting the first tone 2 syllable they hear to the underlying tone 3 syllable /tşu3/ for lexical access (Zhang, Xia, & Peng, 2015). This computational process was operational even on the deviant [tşu2], assigning an underlying tone 3 to it. Hence, no MMN effect was observed since participants treated the deviant as the first syllable of a sandhi standard, focusing their attention on the underlying representation rather than the surface representation.

It is also possible that the lack of an MMN effect in the Sandhi condition could be due to activation of an underspecified tone 3 in Mandarin (Politzer-Ahles, Schluter, Wu, & Almeida, accepted). The featurally underspecified lexicon model (FUL), proposed by Lahiri and Reetz (2002, 2010), claims that there is a single abstract underlying representation for each morpheme stored in the mental lexicon. Phonetic details and predictable phonological variants are not stored. Eulitz and Lahiri (2004) conducted a mismatch negativity study to investigate this underspecification account for vowels. In this study, German vowels [e], [ø], and [o] were used as stimuli, with [e] and [ø] having an underspecified [CORONAL] feature and [o] having a [DORSAL] feature. Six conditions were generated: [e] standard/[o] deviant, [o] standard/[e] deviant, [ø] standard/[o] deviant, [o] standard/[ø] deviant, [e] standard/ [ø] deviant, and [ø] standard/[e] deviant. Their results showed reduced MMN effects for the [e] standard/[o] deviant condition and the [ø] standard/[o] deviant condition compared to the [o] standard/[e] deviant condition and the [o] standard/ [ø] deviant condition, respectively. Moreover, the [e] standard/[ø] deviant condition and the [ø] standard/[e] deviant condition did not elicit different MMN amplitudes. Eulitz and Lahiri (2004) suggested that their results support underspecification for the [CORONAL] feature in German. For the [o] standard condition with either an [ø] or an [e] deviant, the [DORSAL] feature was consistently activated in the underlying representation. When participants encountered the deviant [ø] or [e], the [CORONAL] feature was extracted from the surface representation, contradicting the pre-activated [DORSAL] feature, resulting in a larger MMN amplitude. In contrast, for the [ø] or [e] standard condition with an [o] deviant conditions, the underlying representation of [ø] or [e], which is underspecified, was pre-activated. When participants heard the deviant [o], they extracted the [DORSAL] feature from the surface representation of [o]. This [DORSAL] feature did not conflict with the pre-activated underspecified place feature. Therefore, only a weak conflict was created between the standard (underspecified feature) and deviant ([DORSAL] feature), resulting in a much weaker MMN amplitude.

Cornell, Lahiri, and Eulitz (2011) conducted a follow-up mismatch negativity study to examine the underspecified place feature in complex linguistic structures in which [ø], [e] and [o] were embedded as the first vowel of a disyllabic word ([mø:rən], [me:rən], [mo:rən]). The results showed reduced MMN effects when [mø:rən] served as the standard (i.e., [ø] has the underspecified place feature in the underlying representation) and [mo:rən] served as the deviant compared to when [mø:rən] was the deviant and [mo:rən] was the standard. The results in Cornell, Lahiri, and Eulitz (2011) were consistent with those in Eulitz and Lahiri (2004), suggesting that the [CORONAL] feature in German should be underspecified and German speakers are sensitive to the underlying underspecified place feature not only in isolated words but also in complex words.

The underspecification account may also explain the lack of MMN effects in the Sandhi Condition in the current MMN study. Given that participants were actively predicting the sandhi word [tʂu2 jen3] /tʂu3 jen3/ in the Sandhi condition, they consistently applied a computational mechanism, changing the initial surface tone 2 into an underspecified representation (not an underlying tone 3 under this account), resulting in no MMN effect when the deviant [tʂu2] was encountered. Under this account, whether the participants regarded the deviant [tʂu2] as the first syllable of a standard is not important. Even if the deviant [tʂu2] was not treated as the initial syllable of the sandhi standard, the underspecified representation would still not elicit an MMN effect since the underspecified first syllable of the sandhi standard and the specified deviant [tʂu2] are not in conflict with each other, resulting in no MMN effect.

Politzer-Ahles, Schluter, Wu, & Almeida (accepted) proposed that Mandarin tone 3 is underspecified. In their study, reduced MMN effects were consistently observed when a tone 3 monosyllable was the standard and a tone 1, tone 2, or tone 4 monosyllable was the deviant compared to when a tone 1, tone 2 or tone 4 monosyllable was the standard and a tone 3 monosyllable was the deviant. However, Li and Chen (2015) only found the asymmetric MMN pattern for the tone 2/tone 3 pair but not for the tone 1/tone 3 pair, leading them to conclude that Mandarin tone 3 should be represented as both tone 2 and tone 3 in the mental lexicon rather than as an underspecified tone.

The claim that Mandarin tone 3 is underspecified is not well supported for a number of reasons. First, many underspecified segments, such as coronals, are acquired early in speech sound development. It has been shown that [n] is one of the earliest acquired consonants in English (Kilminster & Laird, 1978; Lynch, Brookshire, & Fox, 1980). However, previous studies on child language acquisition in Mandarin suggest that Mandarin tone 3 is acquired late by children in both perception and production because of its falling and rising fundamental frequency contour (Wong, 2012; Wong, Schwartz, & Jenkins, 2005). Second, for adult Mandarin speakers, the middle of a tone 3 often carries creaky voice, which is an indication of articulatory effort (Chao, 1968). Third, underspecified segments are usually of higher frequency than other segments (Paradis & Prunet, 1991). Based on this, Mandarin tone 3 should have the highest frequency compared to the other tones if it is underspecified. However, it is tone 4 in Mandarin that has the highest type and token frequency. Mandarin tone 3 is only ranked second in terms of type frequency and third with respect to token frequency (Zhang & Lai, 2010). Finally, across many Chinese dialects, not only does Mandarin have the tone 3 versus tone 2 phonological alternation, but many other Chinese dialects have it as well. However, the acoustic realization of tone 3 in these dialects is not always the same as that in Mandarin: a low falling-rising tone for Mandarin T3 (214), but for Tianjin Chinese, T3 → T2/__T3 where T3 is a low-rising tone (24) and T2 is a high-level tone (55) (Chen, 2000; Zhang & Liu, 2015). Therefore, these observations suggest that any explanations using tone 3 characteristics to justify the underspecification of tone 3 are less plausible. Given these concerns, it is premature to conclude that Mandarin tone 3 is underspecified. Although our current MMN results are compatible with both accounts: 1) Mandarin speakers convert the initial tone 2 of Mandarin tone 3 sandhi words into an underlying tone 3 and use the underlying tone 3 for lexical access, and 2) Mandarin tone 3 is underspecified, our psycholinguistic priming data make us lean towards the first account since we found a significant underlying tone priming effect, which suggests that Mandarin tone 3 seems to have a specified underlying tone 3 representation.

To address these issues, mismatch negativity experiments on Southern Min tone sandhi 24 → 33 and 51 → 55 could be illuminating. Based on the current priming and MMN data, we predict that for Southern Min tone sandhi 24 → 33, we may observe an MMN effect in the Tone 33 Condition (similar to the

Tone 2 Condition in the Mandarin MMN experiment) for both high and low frequency words. However, we may not find an MMN effect in the Sandhi Condition (similar to the Sandhi Condition in the Mandarin MMN experiment) for both high and low frequency words because Southern Min sandhi 24 → 33 words are mostly processed based on the underlying representation, which is very similar to how Mandarin tone 3 sandhi words are processed. Therefore, we predict a similar MMN pattern for Southern Min tone sandhi 24 → 33 as found for Mandarin tone 3 sandhi, regardless of sandhi word frequency.

For Southern Min tone sandhi 51 → 55, we also expect to observe an MMN effect in the Tone 55 Condition (similar to the Tone 2 Condition in the Mandarin MMN experiment) for both high and low frequency words. However, we only expect an MMN effect in the Sandhi Condition (similar to the Sandhi Condition in the Mandarin MMN experiment) for low frequency words, and not for high frequency words. Since low frequency Southern Min sandhi 51 → 55 words are processed mostly based on the surface representation, which is very different from the processing of Mandarin tone 3 sandhi words, we predict a distinct MMN pattern for low frequency Southern Min tone sandhi 51 → 55 as compared to the Mandarin tone 3 sandhi. Results of these proposed MMN experiments will shed light on whether it is plausible to posit an underspecified representation for tone sandhi words.

5.3 Models of Spoken Word Recognition

While this book was not designed to directly evaluate

specific assumptions or directly examine the validity of different models of spoken word recognition, our data can shed light on some general issues concerning these models. First, the priming and MMN data in this book are more compatible with models that assume an abstract lexical representation given that our priming and MMN data showed contributions of an underlying representation. Even for Southern Min tone sandhi 51 → 55 in which the surface representation plays a major role, the underlying representation still facilitates processing and contributes to lexical access.

Second, in our Mandarin and Southern Min priming studies, the facilitation effect between the primes and the first syllable of targets suggests morpheme-level facilitation but not cohort competition at the word level. Therefore, a morpheme level must be active in models of spoken word recognition to account for Chinese lexical processing.

Finally, the robust and earlier omission MMN effect in the Tone 2 condition compared to that in the Mix condition is consistent with models assuming that top-down information can influence lexical access since participants were actively predicting the incoming stimuli in the Tone 2 condition (top-down influence) given the predictive context, but failed to do so in the Mix condition. Thus, we observed a stronger and earlier omission MMN effect in the Tone 2 Condition compared to that in the Mix condition, where participants could not predict the incoming stimuli since all the stimuli were different disyllabic words.

5.4 Conclusion

The current book investigated how words undergoing tone sandhi are processed and represented in the mental lexicon. In particular, we examined contributions of the surface and underlying representations to the processing of Mandarin and Southern Min tone sandhi words. Together, the psycholinguistic priming studies and the neurolinguistic MMN study showed that Mandarin tone 3 sandhi words operate in a computational fashion, suggesting that Mandarin speakers access the /tone 3 tone 3/ underlying representation and represent it in the mental lexicon regardless of word frequency. Southern Min tone sandhi words are processed and represented based on both underlying and surface representations, with the relative contribution of each representation varying depending on the characteristics of tone sandhi and frequency. The current experiments document differences in tone sandhi processing within the same language and across different languages.

References

Allopenna, P. D., Magnuson, J. S., & Tanenhaus, M. K. (1998). Tracking the time course of spoken word recognition using eye movements: evidence for continuous mapping models. *Journal of Memory and Language*, *38*, 419-439.

Anderson, J. R. (1996). ACT: a simple theory of complex cognition. *American Psychologist*, *51*(4), 355-365.

Baayen, R. H. (2008). *Analyzing linguistic data: A practical introduction to statistics using R*. Cambridge: Cambridge University Press.

Bates, D., Maechler, M., Bolker, B. M., & Walker, S. (2014). lme4: Linear mixed-effects models using Eigen and S4. *Journal of Statistical Software*. http://arxiv.org/abs/1406.5823.

Bendixen, A., SanMiguel, I., & Schröger, E. (2012). Early electrophysiological indicators for predictive processing in audition: A review. *International Journal of Psychophysiology*, *83*, 120-131.

Bendixen, A., Schröger, E., & Winkler, I. (2009). I heard that coming: event-related potential evidence for stimulus-driven prediction in the auditory system. *Journal of Neuroscience*, *29*, 8447-8451.

Bendixen, A., Scharinger, M., Strauβ, A., & Obleser, J. (2014). Prediction in the service of comprehension: Modulated early brain responses to omitted speech segments. *Cortex*, *53*, 9-26.

Boersma, P., & Weenink, D. (2013). Praat: doing phonetics by computer [Computer program]. Version 5.3.56, retrieved 15 September 2013 from http://www.praat.org/.

Burton, M., Jongman, A., & Sereno, J. (1996). Phonological and orthographic priming effects in auditory and visual word recognition. In W. Ham & L. Lavoie (eds.), *Working Papers of the Cornell Phonetics Laboratory* (Vol. 11, pp.17-41). Ithaca, NY: Cornell University, Department of Linguistics.

Chan, M. K. M., & Ren, H.-M. (1989). Wuxi tone sandhi: from last to first syllable dominance. *Acta Linguistica Hafniensia*, *21*(2), 35-64.

Chandrasekaran, B., Krishnan, A., & Gandour, J. T. (2007). Mismatch negativity to pitch contours is influenced by language experience. *Brain*

Research, *1128*, 148-156.

Chao, Y. (1968). *A Grammar of Spoken Chinese*. Berkeley: University of California Press.

Chen, Matthew Y. (2000). *Tone sandhi: patterns across Chinese dialects*. Cambridge University Press, Cambridge.

Cheng, C.-C., Huang, C.-R., Lo, F.-J., Tsai, M.-C., Huang, Y.-C., Chen, X.-Y., Han, Joyce Y.-C., & Lu, C.-J. (2005). Digital Resources Center for Global Chinese Teaching and Learning, Institute of Linguistics, Academia Sinica. http://elearning.ling.sinica.edu.tw/CWordfreq.html.

Cheng, R. L. (1968). Tone sandhi in Taiwanese. *Linguistics*, *41*, 19-42.

Chien, Y.-F., Sereno, J. A., & Zhang, J. (2016). Priming the representation of Mandarin tone 3 sandhi words. *Language, Cognition and Neuroscience*, *31*, 179-189.

Connine, C. M., Titone, D., Deelman, T., & Blasko, D. (1997). Similarity mapping in spoken word recognition. *Journal of Memory and Language*, *37*, 463-480.

Connine, C. M., Random, L., & Patterson, D. J. (2008). Processing variant forms in spoken word recognition: the role of variant frequency. *Perception and Psychophysics*, *70*(3), 403-411.

Cornell, S., Lahiri, A., & Eulitz, C. (2011). "What you encode is not necessarily what you store": Evidence for sparse feature representations from mismatch negativity. *Brain Research*, *1394*, 79-89.

Cutler, A., & Weber, A. (2007). Listening experience and phonetic-to-lexical mapping in L2. *16th International Congress of Phonetics Sciences*, Dudwailer: Pirrot, 43-48.

DeLong, K. A., Urbach, T. P., & Kutas, M. (2005). Probabilistic word pre-activation during language comprehension inferred from electrical brain activity. *Nature Neuroscience*, *8*(8), doi:10.1038/nn1504.

Dunn, B. R., Dunn, D. A., Languis, M., & Andrew, D. (1998). The relation of ERP components to complex memory processing. *Brain and Cognition*, *36*(3), 355-376.

Eulitz, C., & Lahiri, A. (2004). Neurobiological evidence for abstract phonological representations in the mental lexicon during speech recognition. *Journal of Cognitive Neuroscience*, *16*, 577-583.

Federmeier, K. D. (2007). Thinking ahead: The role and roots of prediction in language comprehension. *Psychophysiology*, *44*, 491-505.

Fiorentino, R., & Fund-Reznicek, E. (2009). Masked morphological priming of compound constituents. *The Mental Lexicon*, *4*, 159-193.
Flege, J. E., Takagi, N., & Mann, V. (1996). Lexical familiarity and English-language experience affect Japanese adults' perception of /ɹ/ and /l/. *The Journal of the Acoustical Society of America*, *99*, 1161-1173.
Goldinger, S. D. (1996). Words and voices: Episodic traces in spoken word identification and recognition memory. *Journal of Experimental Psychology: Learning, Memory, and Cognition*, *22*, 1166-1183.
Goldinger, S. D. (1998). Echoes of echoes? An episodic theory of lexical access. *Psychological Review*, *105*, 251-279.
Goldinger, S. D. (2007). A complementary-system approach to abstract and episodic speech perception. *16th International Congress of Phonetics Sciences*, Dudwailer: Pirrot, 49-54.
Goldinger, S. D., Pisoni, D. B., & Logan, J. S. (1991). On the nature of talker variability effects on recall of spoken word lists. *Journal of Experimental Psychology: Learning, Memory, and Cognition*, *17*, 152-162.
Gu, F., Li, J., Wang, X., Hou, Q., Huang, Y., & Chen, L. (2012). Memory traces for tonal language words revealed by auditory event-related potentials. *Psychophysiology*, *49*, 1353-1360.
Hamburger, M., & Slowiaczek, L. M. (1996). Phonological priming reflects lexical competition. *Psychonomic Bulletin & Review*, *3*, 520-525.
Ho. (2001). Hong Kong, Mainland China and Taiwan: Chinese Character Frequency — a Trans-Regional Diachronic Survey. http://humanum.arts.cuhk.edu.hk/Lexis/chifreq/
Janata, P. (2001). Brain electrical activity evoked by mental formation of auditory expectations and images. *Brain Topography*, *13*, 169-193.
Jongman, A., Sereno, J. A., Raaijmakers, M., & Lahiri, A. (1992). The phonological representation of [voice] in speech perception. *Language and Speech*, *35*(1, 2), 137-152.
Kanzanina, N., Phillips, C., & Idsardi, W. (2006). The influence of meaning on the perception of speech sounds. *Proceedings of the National Academy of Sciences of the United States of America*, *103*(30), 11381-11386.
Kazanina, N., Lau, E. F., Lieberman, M., Yoshida, M., & Phillips, C. (2007). The effect of syntactic constraints on the processing of

backwards anaphora. *Journal of Memory and Language*, *56*, 384-409.

Kilminster, M. G. E., & Laird, E. M. (1978). Articulation development in children aged three to nine years. *Australian Journal of Human Communication Disorders*, *6*(1), 23-30.

Kim, K. H., Kim, J. H., Yoon, J., & Jung, K.-Y. (2008). Influence of task difficulty on the features of event-related potential during visual oddball task. *Neuroscience Letters*, *445*(2), 179-183.

Kiparsky, P. (1973). Abstractness, opacity and global rules. In Fujimura, Osamu (ed.), *Three Dimensions of Linguistic Theory* (pp.57-86), Tokyo Institute for Advanced Studies of Language.

Klatt, D. H. (1979). Speech perception: a model of acoustic-phonetic analysis and lexical access. *Journal of Phonetics*, *7*, 279-312.

Kujala, T., Tervaniemi, M., & Schröger, E. (2007). The mismatch negativity in cognitive and clinical neuroscience: Theoretical and methodological considerations. *Biological Psychology*, *74*, 1-19.

Lahiri, A., Jongman, A., & Sereno, J. A. (1990). The pronominal clitic [dər] in Dutch: A theoretical and experimental approach. In G. E. Booij and J. van Marle (eds.), *Yearbook of Morphology*, *3*, 115-127. Dordrecht: Foris Publications.

Lahiri, A., & Reetz, H. (2002). Underspecified recognition. *Laboratory Phonology*, *7*, 637-675.

Lahiri, A., & Reetz, H. (2010). Distinctive features: phonological underspecification in representation and processing. *Journal of Phonetics*, *38*, 44-59.

Landi, M., Crowley, M. J., Wu, J., Bailey, C. A., & Mayes, L. C. (2012). Deviant ERP response to spoken non-words among adolescents exposed to cocaine in utero. *Brain and Language*, *120*(3), 209-216.

Lau, E. F., Holcomb, P. J., & Kuperberg, G. R. (2013). Dissociating N400 effects of prediction from association in single-word contexts. *Journal of Cognitive Neuroscience*, *25*(3), 484-502.

Lau, E., Stroud, C., Plesch, S., & Phillips, C. (2006). The role of structural prediction in rapid syntactic analysis. *Brain and Language*, *98*, 74-88.

Lee, C.-Y. (2007). Does horse activate mother? Processing lexical tone in form priming. *Language and Speech*, *50*(1), 101-123.

Lee, Y.-J. (2008). *The role of lexical tone in spoken word recognition of Chinese*. Master's thesis, University of Kansas, Kansas, USA.

Li, X., & Chen, Y. (2015). Representation and processing of lexical tone and tonal variants: Evidence from the mismatch negativity. *PLoS ONE* 10(12): e0143097. doi:10.1371/journal.pone.0143097.

Lin, J.-W. (1994). Lexical government and tone group formation in Xiamen Chinese. *Phonology*, *11*, 237-275.

Luce, P. A. (1986). A computational analysis of uniqueness points in auditory word recognition. *Perception and Psychophysics*, *39*, 155-158.

Luce, P. A., & Pisoni, D. B. (1998). Recognition spoken words: the neighborhood activation model. *Ear and Hearing*, *19*, 1-36.

Lynch, J. I., Brookshire, B. L., & Fox, D. R. (1980). A Parent — Child Cleft Palate Curriculum: Developing Speech and Language. CC Publications, Oregon.

Magnuson, J. S., McMurray, B., Tanenhaus, M. K., & Aslin, R. N. (2003). Lexical effects on compensation for coarticulation: the ghost of Christmas past. *Cognitive Science*, *27*, 285-298.

Marslen-Wilson, W. D., & Welsh, A. (1978). Processing interactions and lexical access during word recognition in continuous speech. *Cognitive Psychology*, *10*(1), 29-63.

McClelland, J. L., & Elman, J. L. (1986). The TRACE model of speech perception. *Cognitive Psychology*, *18*, 1-86.

McClelland, J. L., Mirman, D., & Holt, L. L. (2006). Are there interactive processes in speech perception? *Trends in Cognitive Sciences*, *10*, 363-369.

McQueen, J. M. (2003). The ghost of Christmas future: didn't Scrooge learn to be good? Commentary on Magnuson, McMurray, Tanenhaus, and Aslin (2003). *Cognitive Science*, *27*, 795-799.

McQueen, J. M., & Sereno, J. (2005). Cleaving automatic processes from strategic biases in phonological priming. *Memory & Cognition*, *33*(7), 1185-1209.

Moore, C. B., & Jongman, A. (1997). Speaker normalization in the perception of Mandarin Chinese tones. *Journal of the Acoustical Society of America*, *102*, 1864-1877.

Mullennix, J. W., Pisoni, D. B., & Martin, C. S. (1989). Some effects of talker variability on spoken word recognition. *Journal of Acoustical Society of America*, *85*, 365-378.

Näätänen, R., Lehtokoski, A., Lennes, M., Cheour, M., Huotilainen, M., Iivonen, A., Vainio, M., Alku, P., Ilmoniemi, R. J., Luuk, A.,

Allik, J., Sinkkonen, J., & Alho, K. (1997). Language-specific phoneme representations revealed by electric and magnetic brain responses. *Nature*, *385*, 432-434.

Näätänen, R., Paavilainen, P., Rinne, T., & Alho, K. (2007). The mismatch negativity (MMN) in basic research of central auditory processing: a review. *Clinical Neurophysiology*, *118*, 2544-2590.

Näätänen, R., & Winkler, I. (1999). The concept of auditory stimulus representation in neuroscience. *Psychological Bulletin*, *125*, 826-859.

Norman, K., & O'Reilly, R. (2003). Modeling hippocampal and neocortical contributions to recognition memory: a complementary learning system approach. *Psychological Review*, *110*, 611-646.

Norris, D. (1994). Shortlist: a connectionist model of continuous speech recognition. *Cognition*, *52*, 234-289.

Norris, D., & McQueen, J. M. (2008). Shortlist B: a Bayesian model of continuous speech recognition. *Psychological Review*, *115*, 357-395.

Norris, D., McQueen, J. M., & Cutler, A. (2000). Merging information in speech recognition: feedback is never necessary. *Behavioral and Brain Sciences*, *23*, 299-370.

Norris, D., McQueen, J. M., & Cutler, A. (2003). Perceptual learning in speech. *Cognitive Psychology*, *47*, 204-238.

Norris, D., McQueen, J. M., Cutler, A., & Butterfield, S. (1997). The possible-word constraint in the segmentation of continuous speech. *Cognitive Psychology*, *34*, 191-243.

Oldfield, R. C. (1971). The assessment and analysis of handedness: The Edinburgh inventory. *Neuropsychologia*, *9*(1), 97-113.

Paradis, C., & Prunet, J. (1991). Introduction: asymmetry and visibility in consonant articulations. In C. Paradis & J. Prunet (eds.), *The Special Status of Coronals, Internal and External Evidence*, 1-28. San Diego: Academic Press.

Peng, S.-H. (2000). Lexical versus "phonological" representations of Mandarin tones. *Acquisition and the Lexicon*, ed. By Michael B. Broe & Janet B. Pierrehumbert, 152-167. Papers in Laboratory Phonology 5. Cambridge & New York: Cambridge University Press.

Phillips, C., Pellathy, T., Marantz, A., Yellin, E., Wexler, K., Poeppel, D., McGinnis, M., & Roberts, T. (2000). Auditory cortex accesses phonological categories: An MEG mismatch study. *Journal of Cognitive Neuroscience*, *12*(6), 1038-1055.

Politzer-Ahles, S., Schluter, K., Wu, K., & Almeida, D. (accepted). *Journal of Experimental Psychology: Human Perception & Performance.*

Politzer-Ahles, S., & Zhang, J. (in press). Evidence for the role of tone sandhi in Mandarin speech production. *Journal of Chinese Linguistics.*

Radeau, M., Morais, J., & Segui, J. (1995). Phonological priming between monosyllabic spoken words. *Journal of Experimental Psychology: Human Perception & Performance*, *21*, 1297-1311.

Raij, T., McEvoy, L., Mäkelä, J.P., & Hari, R. (1997). Human auditory cortex is activated by omissions of auditory stimuli. *Brain Research*, *745*, 134-143.

Reetz, H., & Jongman, A. (2009). *Phonetics: Transcription, Production, Acoustics, and Perception.* Wiley-Blackwell.

Ren, G.-Q., Yang, Y., & Li, X. (2009). Early cortical processing of linguistic pitch patterns as revealed by the mismatch negativity. *Neuroscience*, *162*, 87-95.

Salverda, A. P., Dahan, D., Tanenhaus, M. K., Crosswhite, K., Masharov, M., & McDonough, J. (2007). Effects of prosodically modulated sub-phonetic variation on lexical competition. *Cognition*, *105*, 466-476.

Scharenborg, O., & Boves, L. (2010). Computational modelling of spoken-word recognition processes: design choices and evaluation. *Pragmatics & Cognition*, *18*, 136-164.

Selkirk, E., & Shen, T. (1990). Prosodic domains in Shanghai Chinese. *The Phonology-Syntax Connection*, 313-337.

Sereno, J. A., & Lee, H. (2015). The contribution of segmental and tonal information in Mandarin spoken word processing. *Language and Speech*, *58*(2), 131-151.

Shei, C. (2014). *Understanding the Chinese Language: A Comprehensive Linguistic Introduction.* Routledge.

Shen, J., Deutsch, D., & Rayner, K. (2013). On-line perception of Mandarin tone 2 and 3: Evidence from eye movements. *Journal of the Acoustical Society of America*, *133*(5), 3016-3029.

Slowiaczek, L. M., McQueen, J. M., Soltano, E. G., & Lynch, M. (2000). Phonological representations in prelexical speech processing: Evidence from form-based priming. *Journal of Memory & Language*, *43*, 530-560.

Smith, E. E., Shoben, E. J., & Rips, L. J. (1974). Structure and process in semantic memory: a featural model for semantic decisions. *Psychological Review*, *81*, 214-241.

Stowe, L. A. (1986). Parsing WH-constructions: evidence for on-line gap location. *Language, Cognition and Neuroscience*, *1*(3), 227-245.

Taft, M., & Chen, H.-C. (1992). Judging homophony in Chinese: The influence of tones. In H.-C. Chen & O.J.L. Tzeng (eds.), *Language Processing in Chinese* (pp.151-172). Amsterdam, the Netherlands: Elsevier.

Tagliaferri, B. (2015). Paradigm. Perception Research Systems, Inc. www.perceptionresearchsystems.com.

Tsao, F.-F., & Yao, R. S. (ed.). (2011). *Online Taiwanese Dictionary*. Ministry of Education, Taipei, Taiwan. 曹逢甫，姚荣松.（编辑）.（2011）. 台湾闽南语常用辞典.

Tsay, J. S., & Myers, J. (2013). *Taiwanese Spoken Corpus*. Department of Linguistics, National Chung Cheng University, Taiwan. 蔡素娟，麦杰,（2013）. 台湾闽南语口语语料库, 台湾中正大学语言学研究所.

Vitevitch, M. S., & Luce, P. A. (1998). Levels of processing in perception of spoken words. *Psychological Science*, *9*(4), 325-329.

Vitevitch, M. S., & Luce, P. A. (1999). Probabilistic phonotactics and neighborhood activation in spoken word recognition. *Journal of Memory and Language*, *40*, 374-408.

Wang, W., & Li, K.-P. (1967). Tone 3 in Pekingese. *Journal of Speech and Hearing Research*, *10*, 629-636.

Wang, X.-D., Gu, F., He, K., Chen, L.-H., & Chen, L. (2012). Preattentive extraction of abstract auditory rules in speech sound stream: A mismatch negativity study using lexical tones. *Public Library of Science (PLoS ONE)*, *7*(1): e30027. Doi: 10.1371/journal.pone.0030027.

Weber, A., & Scharenborg, O. (2012). Models of spoken-word recognition. *WIREs Cogn Sci*, *3*, 387-401.

Wong, P. (2012). Acoustic characteristics of three-year-olds' correct and incorrect monosyllabic Mandarin lexical tone productions. *Journal of Phonetics*, *40*, 141-151.

Wong, P., Schwartz, R., & Jenkins, J. (2005). Perception and production of lexical tones by 3-year-old, Mandarin-speaking children. *Journal of Speech, Language, and Hearing Research*, *48*, 1065-1079.

Xi, J., Zhang, L., Shu, H., Zhang, Y., & Li, P. (2010). Categorical perception of lexical tones in Chinese revealed by mismatch negativity. *Neuroscience*, *170*, 223-231.

Yabe, H., Tervaniemi, M., Reinikainen, K., & Näätänen, R. (1997). Temporal window of integration revealed by MMN to sound omission. *Neuroreport*, *8*, 1971-1974.

Yabe, H., Tervaniemi, M., Sinkkonen, J., Huotilainen, M., Ilmoniemi, R.J., & Näätänen, R. (1998). Temporal window of integration of auditory information in the human brain. *Psychophysiology*, *35*, 615-619.

Ye, Y., & Connine, C. M. (1999). Processing spoken Chinese: the role of tone information. *Language and Cognitive Processes*, *14*, 609-630.

Yuan, J. H., & Chen, Y. (2014). 3rd tone sandhi in Standard Chinese: A corpus approach. *Journal of Chinese Linguistics*, *42*(1), 218-237.

Zhang, C., Xia, Q., & Peng, G. (2015). Mandarin third tone sandhi requires more effortful phonological encoding in speech production: Evidence from an ERP study. *Journal of Neurolinguistics*, *33*, 149-162.

Zhang, J., & Lai, Y.-W. (2008). Phonological knowledge beyond the lexicon in Taiwanese double reduplication. In: Hsiao, Y.-C.E., Hsu, H.-C., Wee, L.-H., Ho, D.-A. (eds.), *Interfaces in Chinese Phonology: Festschrift in Honor of Matthew Y. Chen on His 70th Birthday*. Academia Sinica, Taiwan, 183-222.

Zhang, J., & Lai, Y.-W. (2010). Testing the role of phonetic knowledge in Mandarin tone sandhi. *Phonology*, *27*(1), 153-201.

Zhang, J., Lai, Y.-W., & Sailor, C. (2011). Modeling Taiwanese speakers' knowledge of tone sandhi in reduplication. *Lingua*, *121*, 181-206.

Zhang, J., & Liu, J. (2011). Tone sandhi and tonal coarticulation in Tianjin Chinese. *Phonetica*, *68*(3), 161-191.

Zhang, J., & Liu, J. (2014). The productivity of variable disyllabic tone sandhi in Tianjin Chinese. *Journal of East Asian Linguistics*.

Zheng, H.-Y., Minett, J. W., Peng, G., & Wang, W. S.-Y. (2012). The impact of tone systems on the categorical perception of lexical tones: An event-related potentials study. *Language and Cognitive Processes*, *27*(2), 184-209.

Zhou, X., & Marslen-Wilson, W. D. (1994). Words, morphemes, and syllables in the Chinese mental lexicon. *Language and Cognitive Processes*, *9*, 393-422.

Zhou, X., & Marslen-Wilson, W. D. (1995). Morphological Structure in the Chinese mental lexicon. *Language and Cognitive Processes*, *10*(6), 545-600.

Zhou, X., & Marslen-Wilson, W. D. (1997). The abstractness of phonological representation in the Chinese mental lexicon. In H.-C. Chen (ed.). *Cognitive Processing of Chinese and other Asian Languages* (pp.3-26), Hong Kong: The Chinese University Press.

Appendix 1
Critical Target Mandarin Tone 3 Sandhi Stimuli

High frequency tone 3 sandhi targets

Target	Pinyin	Log Word Frequency	LogFirstSyllable Frequency T2 + T3	LogSecondSyllable Frequency
以往	yi3 wang3	2.64	3.73	2.78
只有	zhi3 jiu3	3.07	3.59	3.84
演讲	yan3 jiang3	2.71	3.37	2.43
也许	ye3 xu3	2.97	3.50	2.86
主管	zhu3 guan3	3.02	3.20	3.00
处理	chu3 li3	3.28	3.11	3.49
想法	xiang3 fa3	2.66	3.30	3.15
引起	yin3 qi3	3.00	2.90	3.15
产品	chan3 pin3	3.39	2.75	2.68
辅导	fu3 dao3	2.73	3.20	2.84
采取	cai3 qu3	2.77	3.16	2.79
彼此	bi3 ci3	2.85	2.94	3.18
选举	xuan3 ju3	2.77	2.89	2.58
保险	bao3 xian3	2.56	2.77	2.64
领导	Ling3 dao3	2.79	2.98	2.83

Low frequency tone 3 sandhi targets

Target	Pinyin	Log Word Frequency	LogFirstSyllable Frequency T2 + T3	LogSecondSyllable Frequency
乞讨	qi3 tao3	1.11	3.60	2.26
厂长	chang3 zhang3	1.20	3.48	2.64
体检	ti3 jian3	1.20	3.36	2.77
喜酒	xi3 jiu3	1.32	3.12	3.02
扭转	niu3 zhuan3	1.76	2.22	2.53
显眼	xian3 yan3	1.23	2.85	2.89
脚本	jiao3 ben3	1.30	2.75	3.09
海产	hai3 chan3	1.15	3.31	2.68
雅典	ya3 dian3	1.32	2.72	2.97
可口	ke3 kou3	1.59	3.42	2.72
打手	da3 shou3	1.00	2.97	3.07
审理	shen3 li3	1.69	2.87	3.49
赌场	du3 chang3	1.48	2.99	3.85
婉转	wan3 zhuan3	1.28	2.99	2.53
养老	yang3 lao3	1.15	2.96	2.95

Appendix 2
Mandarin Disyllabic Filler Word Target Stimuli with Prime Words. Also, Disyllabic Nonword Target Stimuli with Prime Words

Filler words

tie1-tie1xin1, guan1-guan1men2, tou1-ba2guan4, lio1-su2qi4, ling1-shou2shi4, mao1-mao3ding1, qiao1-qiao3yan2, pao1-pao3lu4, shao1-shi3yong4, shai1-ku3qing2, shang1-kou3she2, tong1-shau4ye2, shou1-shang4tai2, xing1-duo4xing4, ma2-gu1qie3, hong2-ji1ben3, qiao2-hu1qi4, pao2-pao2xiao4, yan2-yan2liao4, quan2-quan2shen1, shou2-shou3zhen1, shu2-shu3tiao2, chao2-chao3jia4, ting2-zhen3tou2, tiao2-xue3kuo2, qian2-po3xing2, liao2-ru4kou3, mei2-zong4ku3, ming2-luo4tuo2, dian3-shu1zhuang1, ku3-gao1zhang3, bu3-qian1shou3, ren3-tiao2zhong3, ling3-han2leng3, shui3-lan2se4, zhu3-zhu3yao4, ran3-ran3se4, chuang3-chuang3dang4, ma3-ren4zhen1, qiang3-shui4jiao4, ku3-ling4wai4, da4-da1che1, jiang4-jiang1jun1, hu4-tian1jia1, dong4-ting1ke1, kua4-xing1qiu2, fang4-fan2jian1, ben4-liao2tian1, ban4-ming2men2, xue4-qi2shi2, yuan4-yuan2lai2, wan4-wan3an1, pin4-pin3de2, kao4-hu3ren2, bao4-gui3guai4, kan4-guo3dong4, huo4-huo3ban4, ju4-ju4ji2, fan4-fan4wan3, huan4-huan4qi4

Non-words

fei1-fei1kong1, tan1-tan1lian2, yao1-yao1kao3, chong1-

chong1qian4, han1-han2liu1, fen1-fen2ba3, su1-su2shi3, kuang1-yin2mei3, ke1-lai2qian3, xiu1-mang2zhu3, qing1-qing3mei2, shai1-shai3ku1, zao1-zao3shai4, kan1-mu3kan1, zhou1-sa3pang2, tui1-kan3nen4, kai1-kai4tang1, mi1-mi4shu3, jang1-yan-g4lian4, xiao1-fen4mi1, fu1-pang4ba2, tian1-kong4nian3, qi2-qi1shou1, xia2-xia1yin2, zhai2-zhai1li3, chuan2-qi1pu2, bo2-pi1tao3, chen2-zhuo1gou4, rao2-rao2jia3, zei2-zei2quan3, yin2-yin2da3, bie2-bie2gui3, wen2-wen2pu3, chao2-chao3ren4, luo2-luo3ba2, yao2-yao3bei4, fo2-pu3shua1, ba2-shu3wen2, qiou2-man3li4, chuang2-chuang4ni3, tu2-tu4hua1, miao2-shi4sui1, qiang2-yun4lin2, zhao2-di4xiou3, gong3-gong1miao3, huang3-huang1he4, yuan3-peng1shao2, suo3-gan1niao3, li3-sou1fa4, chou3-chou2tong3, wei3-wei2bian3, er3-er2zhi3, jie3-nu2ai3, ji3-chu2gu3, ban3-mi2kou3, bao3-bao3qu1, kong3-kong3zha1, chuang3-chuang3qing2, zou3-zou3ya4, yao3-yao3dian4, lao3-lao4ti2, niao3-niao4an4, can3-can4shou1, bei3-shi4tu1, rao3-deng4tai2, kao3-gu4shu3, si4-xi1ma2, shang4-shang1wen3, tou4-dou1ku4, shan4-guo1chu2, fu4-shan1zou3, mi4-tang1yin4, men4-men2lian3, da4-da2ai3, mo4-shu2si3, shou4-ni2wan3, tai4-zhe2gan3, qian4-qian3shei2, ba4-ba3kan1, chang4-chang3ku4, wo4-jian3lao1, xiou4-geng3fa2, xia4-zhen3bu4, zhang4-zhang4qu1, du4-du4mai2, mu4-mu4nian2, si4-si4bei3, lu4-lu4bi4, can4-can4wa4

Appendix 3
Critical Target Southern Min Sandhi Stimuli

Taiwanese sandhi 51 → 55 targets

Target	Pinyin	Averaged Familiarity
改途	kai55 too24	5.50
翻船	ping55 tsun24	5.69
保持	po55 tshi24	6.67
补强	poo55 kiong24	5.22
点名	tiam55 mia24	6.92
党团	tang55 thuan24	4.67
鬼神	kui55 sin24	5.56
体能	the55 ling24	5.50
短期	te55 ki24	6.00
主持	tsu55 tshi24	6.69
狗牙	kau55 ge24	2.56
减肥	kiam55 pui24	6.92
枕头	tsim55 thau24	7.00
拣茶	king55 te24	3.19
股权	koo55 khuan24	5.14
转型	tsuan55 hing24	5.31
本钱	pun55 tsinn24	6.78
口琴	khau55 khim24	4.61

Taiwanese sandhi 24 → 33 targets

Target	Pinyin	Averaged Familiarity
排解	pai33 kai51	6.17
培养	pue33 jong51	6.56
平等	ping33 ting51	4.36
茶馆	te33 kuan51	4.08
前景	tsian33 king51	3.64
场所	tiunn33 soo51	6.75
冲水	tshiang33 tsui51	5.97
台长	tai33 tiunn51	4.03
铜管	tang33 kong51	4.78
投保	tau33 po51	5.39
条款	tiau33 khuan51	4.53
逃走	to33 tsau51	6.19
奇巧	ki33 kha51	5.81
钱鬼	tsinn33 kui51	5.92
才子	tsai33 tsu51	5.78
桥顶	kio33 ting51	6.56
从此	tsiong33 tshu51	5.67
平手	penn33 tshiu51	6.25

Appendix 4
Southern Min Disyllabic Filler Word Target Stimuli with Prime Words. Also, Disyllabic Nonword Target Stimuli with Prime Words

Filler words

tse55-tse21tshia55, tshing51-tshing21sann55, sia33-sia21khu55, tong55-tong21pong24, tso24-tso21sing24, tiong33-tiong21bin24, tsing55-tsing21tso33, su51-su21bu33, si33-si21hong33, siu24-siu21ke21, sin33-sin21tsi21, sia55-sia21tsinn21, siu33-siu21hiam51, siong21-siong21ku51, pue24-pue21king51, tshiunn55-tshiunn51kua55, tsau51-tsau51kha55, kiu24-kiu51ping55, tshai51-tshai51thau24, than24-than51tsinn24, thai55-thai51ping24, tai51-tai51tong33, tan24-tan51tiau33, tsi55-tsi51guan33, tshu33-tshu51kua21, tui24-tui51hiong21, tsiau51-tsiau51koo21, thiau33-thiau51bu51, tshio21-tshio51si51, tse51-tse51tian51, ka55-sin21tsi21, tse55-sa33tsinn24, tshi55-kuai33ka51, tsio55-pan21kong55, tso55-tin51tiunn51, tshue55-pai51hue33, pan33-tsing51bing24, phoo33-kuan55tse21, phe33-kun55tsui51, pun33-bio21kong55, se33-pi21hun33, thai33-ku51tiam51, phin24-kam55khai21, kam24-pi55tshu51, pi24-se21se21, su24-kin21tshin55, se24-tsiong51lang24, siong24-tshan51lan33, sia21-phoo55phian21, tsi21-kho51suann55, tshu21-phin55kuan51, tso21-sim33tng24, tsing21-tshau33puann24, tsiam21-tshong51tso33, tshenn51-

Appendix 4   Southern Min Disyllabic Filler Word Target Stimuli with Prime   173
Words. Also, Disyllabic Nonword Target Stimuli with Prime Words

khiam33pi55, sim51-pan55too24, tshau51-ping55kue21, bue51-tsa33boo51, tiong51-pa21tshi33, bong51-tsing21sang21

Non-words

siann55-siann55ting24, tse55-tse55tsinn24, sai55-sai55too24, khai55-khai55gong24, kau55-kau55pau24, tsam55-tsam55si24, pang33-pang33thong51, tshiunn33-tshiunn33tsuan51, pa33-pa33bio51, gan33-gan33gun51, tsan33-tsan33si51, si33-si33kann51, tsau24-tsau33to51, pe24-pe33king51, phenn24-phenn33pan51, bi24-bi33pang51, sia24-sia33tiam51, tiam24-tiam33kai51, tiann24-tiann21gu33, tiau24-tiau21kui21, sim24-sim21giam33, poo24-poo51tsai55, tuann24-tuann51tshiam55, kiam24-kiam51bing55, khue24-khue51gu33, thiong21-thiong55biau24, tsiu21-tsiu55thing24, tshiunn21-tshiunn55pu24, kenn21-kenn55tam24, sing21-sing55tshiu24, kue21-kue55si24, sue21-sue33thang51, kua21-kua33gua51, tuan21-tuan33kam51, koo21-koo33kiau51, kong21-kong33the51, song21-song33tsiunn51, pa21-pa21tiam21, tsing21-tsing51bio33, ta51-ta55thuan24, tshai51-tshai55tshi24, san51-san55sun24, binn51-binn55tai24, tiong51-tiong55sin24, kiong51-kiong55bin24, tso51-tso21tsio55, tong51-tong21too33, kua51-kua51ti33, kuai51-kuai51tinn55, tiunn51-tiunn51kiann21, tshuan51-tshuan51kiong55, pue51-pue51phue55, thiam55-thiam21to55, thiann55-thiann21king33, thong55-thong21ko55, to55-to21khi21, tui55-tui51guan33, siu55-siu51te24, siong55-siong51sing21, sia33-sia21sun33, tann33-tann21kang55, tsam33-tsam21kian21, bin33-bin21tsiann21, phong33-phong21siau21, pian33-pian51tenn33, ke33-ke51tsu55, pha55-tiunn33poo55, kam55-siunn33kau55, tham55-tsoo21ku33, siau55-koo21king55, phiau55-tsong51tsai33, kin55-kuan51ting33, tshiu33-tam55too33, pu33-tsan55kuan33, ku33-thin21siong33, pio33-tham21tshua21, pong33-kai51kang33, tsau33-too51png33, thin24-pong55phua21, kuan24-pio55phinn21, tsong24-pu21bang33, tam24-kin21kan55, tsan24-kinn51phuann33, phang24-tshui51tong33, pai21-se55sai55, tham21-tshiu55siann55, tsam21-tho33khi21, tshu21-pa33tsai55, tshua21-tso51kin33, kinn21-tu51kho55, tiunn51-phang55sang21, siunn51-tsha55tshing55, po51-pha33po33, tho51-kam33pan55, koo51-tshu21bang33, tu51-pai21sing55

Appendix 5

Acoustic Details of the Seven Standard [tşu2] Tokens, the Seven Standard [tşu3] Tokens and the Deviant [tşu2] (measured in Hz, rounded to the nearest integer)

Standard [tşu2]

Time (% of tone)	0%	10%	20%	30%	40%	50%	60%	70%	80%	90%	100%
[tşu2] (1)	161	161	159	157	158	162	169	179	190	202	210
[tşu2] (2)	168	167	164	160	160	162	169	179	190	201	207
[tşu2] (3)	172	169	165	159	156	157	162	171	183	192	198
[tşu2] (4)	168	167	165	165	171	183	197	211	224	234	236
[tşu2] (5)	169	166	162	157	154	154	157	162	170	180	191
[tşu2] (6)	173	176	163	154	151	150	151	154	162	172	181
[tşu2] (7)	159	155	152	148	148	150	155	161	170	183	197
Mean	167	166	161	157	157	160	166	174	184	195	203
SD	5	6	4	5	7	11	14	17	19	19	16

Standard [tşu3]

Time (% of tone)	0%	10%	20%	30%	40%	50%	60%	70%	80%	90%	100%
[tşu3] (1)	160	158	153	146	140	136	132	129	126	125	125
[tşu3] (2)	171	167	159	149	141	133	126	122	119	117	118

continued

Time (% of tone)	0%	10%	20%	30%	40%	50%	60%	70%	80%	90%	100%
[tʂu3] (3)	165	157	153	147	140	133	129	126	125	124	124
[tʂu3] (4)	173	167	160	151	143	137	131	125	122	121	122
[tʂu3] (5)	171	176	162	151	143	135	129	124	122	122	122
[tʂu3] (6)	163	158	155	150	144	138	133	128	126	124	124
[tʂu3] (7)	170	164	158	151	144	140	137	133	129	126	125
Mean	168	164	157	149	142	136	131	127	124	123	123
SD	5	6	3	2	2	2	3	3	3	3	2

Deviant [tʂu2]

Time (% of tone)	0%	10%	20%	30%	40%	50%	60%	70%	80%	90%	100%
[tʂu2] (1)	159	159	151	145	144	147	154	165	179	194	200

图书在版编目(CIP)数据

基于启动和脑电波实验研究普通话和闽南语连读变调词的储存模式＝Priming and ERP Investigations on the Processing and Representation of the Tonal Alternations in Mandain Chinese and Southern Min Dialect：英文/钱昱夫著. —上海：复旦大学出版社，2019.6
ISBN 978-7-309-14280-8

Ⅰ.①基… Ⅱ.①钱… Ⅲ.①普通话-变调-研究-英文②闽南话-变调-研究-英文 Ⅳ.①H116.4②H177.2

中国版本图书馆 CIP 数据核字(2019)第 079005 号

基于启动和脑电波实验研究普通话和闽南语连读变调词的储存模式
钱昱夫　著
责任编辑/方尚芩

复旦大学出版社有限公司出版发行
上海市国权路 579 号　邮编：200433
网址：fupnet@ fudanpress.com　http://www.fudanpress.com
门市零售：86-21-65642857　团体订购：86-21-65118853
外埠邮购：86-21-65109143　出版部电话：86-21-65642845
江苏凤凰数码印务有限公司

开本 890×1240　1/32　印张 6　字数 143 千
2019 年 6 月第 1 版第 1 次印刷

ISBN 978-7-309-14280-8/H·2895
定价：36.00 元

如有印装质量问题，请向复旦大学出版社有限公司出版部调换。
版权所有　侵权必究